Scholastic World Cultures

LATIN AMERICA

by James A. Hudson
and David Goddy

FOURTH EDITION

Consultant

A. CURTIS WILGUS, Ph.D.

Director, Pan American Foundation, Inc.
Former Professor of History and Director of the School of
Inter-American Studies, University of Florida.

 SCHOLASTIC INC.

ISBN 0-590-34747-0

James A. Hudson is a former news editor of United Press International and author of several books including *RFK: 1925-1968* (Scholastic). David Goddy is managing editor of Scholastic *Update*. Both have traveled extensively in Latin America.

Publisher: Eleanor Angeles
Editorial Director for WORLD CULTURES: *Carolyn Jackson*
Assistant Editor: Elise Bauman

Art Director and Designer: Irmgard Lochner
Art Assistant: Wilhelmina Reyinga
Photo Editor: Elnora Bode

COVER: In the Peruvian city of Cuzco, "down the stone-paved lanes built by their Inca ancestors, Indian women trudge wearing layers of long skirts and carrying big bundles in their shawls."

—Chapter 16

LATIN
AMERICA

Table of Contents

LATIN AMERICA

UNITED STATES

ATLANTIC OCEAN

MEXICO

HISPANIOLA

CUBA

PUERTO RICO

CENTRAL AMERICA

CARIBBEAN SEA

GUYANA

VENEZUELA

SURINAM

FRENCH GUIAN

COLOMBIA

ECUADOR

BRAZIL

PACIFIC OCEAN

PERU

BOLIVIA

PARAGUAY

CHILE

URUGUAY

ARGENTINA

ఆక "This world of ours is not merely an accident of geography. Our continents are bound together by a common history— the endless exploration of new frontiers. Our nations are the product of a common struggle—the revolt from colonial rule. And our people share a common heritage—the quest for dignity and the freedom of man."

PRESIDENT JOHN F. KENNEDY, *1962-1965*, ON U.S. TIES TO LATIN AMERICA

PROLOGUE

RESTLESS LAND

WHAT'S THE IMAGE of Latin America you've gotten from U.S. movies, TV, radio, newspapers, and magazines? Is it of a slow, easygoing place, where people take long *siestas** (naps) and put off their work until *manana** (tomorrow)? Of a sunny land of palm trees, sandy beaches, and resort hotels? Of a violent region where iron-fisted dictators battle guerrilla fighters?

Such images make proud Latin Americans feel frustrated. They wish North Americans paid closer attention to their region, and understood it better. Put yourself in their shoes, and you can easily understand their concern. As the only big world power in the Western hemisphere, the U.S. has enormous political and economic influence on nearly every nation in Latin America. Many depend on U.S. investments and loans to keep their economies going. So, just about every Latin American government tries hard to keep friendly ties with its giant North American neighbor.

Strong ties are just as important to the U.S. as they are to Latin America. Economically, Latin America makes up a huge market for U.S. goods and services, and supplies our industries with many needed raw materials, especially oil from Mexico and Venezuela. And because Latin America is so close to the U.S., our leaders often worry that political turmoil in the region might undermine U.S. security.

For instance, many Americans today worry about the touchy situation in Central America, particularly in Nicaragua. That nation's alliance with Cuba and the Soviet Union has alarmed many who fear the spread of Communist influence in the area. In 1986, opinion polls showed that a majority of U.S. citizens opposed sending U.S. troops. Many experts say the region's deepest problem is poverty, not politics.

Such issues show why Americans need to know all they can about Latin America. This book takes you on a fascinating tour of this colorful and complex region. You'll visit modern cities and traditional villages. You'll see how young people live in the midst of tropical rain forests and atop remote mountains. You'll hear firsthand accounts of why some people, in desperation, turn to revolution. You'll see that Latin America is very different from many of its stereotypes.

One fascinating difference is language. The official language of most Latin American countries is Spanish, but Brazil's 125 million people speak Portuguese, not Spanish. Even among the Spanish-speaking countries of Latin America, the way people speak varies widely. An Argentinian may find it very hard to understand the Spanish spoken by, say, a Puerto Rican.

Geography is another major difference. The shepherd of Argentina's Patagonia region, the southernmost part of Latin America, undergoes winters almost as severe as those in the United States. The villager living

Latin faces vary: a white Chilean college girl (top left), a Peruvian Indian (top right), a mestizo girl in Colombia (bottom left), and a black teenager in Haiti.

on Mexico's central plateau may go through a whole winter without seeing a snowflake. Since these regions are on the opposite side of the Equator, they don't have winters at the same time of the year. And any winter at all would be strange to a resident of northern Brazil or Ecuador who lives on the Equator.

Although the differences between Latin Americans are very great, there are still many things that most Latin Americans have in common. The name, Latin America, for example, indicates that the people of the region share a common background. Their languages, customs, religion, and art come mainly from Spain, Portugal, and France. The cultures of these three countries, in turn, were based on that of ancient Rome. Since the Roman language was Latin —and Spanish, Portuguese, and French come from Latin—the people who form this Latin culture in the Americas are called Latin Americans.

Beyond the bonds of language and culture, there is poverty. Most Latin Americans are poor whether in a dusty Indian village in Bolivia, or a Brazilian shantytown. Many of them are desperately poor. But not everyone is poor—and this is another common thread throughout Latin America. In every country, there is a small group of well-to-do, cultured, educated, widely traveled people—government officials, business people, college professors, ranchers, doctors, priests, and army officers. They make up about two percent of Latin America's population, but they own about 70 percent of the wealth. Usually, these are the people who run Latin American governments. The army officers often play an especially large role in running the governments. In the U.S., by contrast, the military must stay out of politics.

Finally, many Latin Americans share a life of isolation. Throughout the area, millions of people live their lives with very little contact with the world outside their villages. Rarely do they travel beyond the closest district market. They do not write letters to friends or relatives, and they do not make telephone calls to other villages.

This is not by choice. People live isolated lives because of poverty. Often people don't write letters because they don't know how to write. Besides, poor people don't have money for such luxuries as TV sets, radios, telephones, and magazines. Roads are often bad, and even if they were better, who could afford a car? Many of these people know little beyond what is happening in their own village. They will probably live out their lives in the village in which they were born.

Yet things are changing in rural Latin America. Roads are being improved. Electricity and running water have been brought into many villages. More people are buying radios and tape players. Most still cannot afford a television. But even in remote villages in the Andes Mountains, people may go to a public square in the evenings to watch TV on a set bought by the village council. Or perhaps they crowd around a set left on in a store window, or gather to watch in a neighbor's parlor.

In these villages, the people have begun to discover that not everyone else in the world is as poor as they are. They are learning that there may be jobs in the big cities, and the chance to earn much more money than they thought possible. Millions of Latin Americans are leaving their villages in search of jobs and a new kind of life. Sometimes they find the jobs. Often they are sorely disappointed for the cities cannot provide jobs

13

With an eye on the past and an ear to the
future, this Indian girl of Guatemala works
on her ancient loom while a transistor radio
at her knee blares out sounds of today.

for all the people who are flooding in.

Despite its great poverty and many other problems, Latin America's future is not all grim. In fact, perhaps the biggest recent change is the wave of democracy that has swept the region. Since 1979, one dozen major nations in Latin America have shifted from military rule to elected governments. Today, an estimated 94 percent of the region's over 400 million people live in democratic nations.

This encouraging trend reminds us that the U.S. and Latin America share many bonds. Historically, they were both symbols of a new world of opportunity and hope for European explorers and settlers. Another shared bond is their struggle for independence from their colonial rulers. Most Latin Americans share with their northern neighbors a belief in the republican-democratic form of government.

To be sure, there's much that's different in Latin America. As visitors to the region quickly learn, Latin America offers a diverse landscape and same unique ways of life. Latin Americans are as interesting, complex, and varied as people in the United States—perhaps more. Read on, and you'll find out why.

1
MEXICO

Chapter 1

Gateway to Latin America

IN SPANISH, Rio Grande* means "Big River." Despite its impressive name, the Rio Grande is hardly more than a trickle during certain times of the year. At these times, a person can cross the river without wetting his ankles. But, in the spring, the rains come, and the river bed fills up and runs swiftly to the Gulf of Mexico. Then the Rio Grande truly becomes the Big River, a worthy international dividing line between the U.S. and Mexico.

What kind of country lies across the line? It is a land of sharply rising mountains and steep ravines; of mile-high cities and low, sultry jungles. It is a land where a volcano can suddenly erupt out of a hill one day and grow to be a mountain within a few months. It is a land where ancient ruins can lie unknown beneath a jungle cover for centuries.

There is a story that when the Spanish first conquered Mexico four hundred years ago, a Spanish nobleman recently back from Mexico was summoned before the king of Spain who was curious about his new domain. "What kind of a land is it?" the king

17

asked. The nobleman struggled with words but could find none adequate. Finally, he took a piece of paper and crumpled it in his hand. He squeezed it until it was a jagged ball of ridges and seams and showed it to the king. "Sire," he said, "there is a map of your new land."

☆　☆　☆　☆　☆　☆　☆　☆　☆

Miguel* is a teenager who lives in Mexico City. He is a bright boy but a poor student. He reads a lot, but mostly comic books and the comic strips in the daily newspaper. He also watches U.S. television programs, such as "Dallas." On Mexican television, such shows are "dubbed," or translated, into Spanish, for Spanish is the language of Mexico and of most other countries of Latin America.

Miguel likes to go to movies, to play a guitar, and to dream some day of becoming rich and famous. He hopes to become so, not as a businessman, doctor, lawyer — nor even as a ballplayer. He dreams of becoming a *matador,** a professional bullfighter.

Whenever Miguel and his friends get a chance, they sneak into the Plaza México, a huge arena where bullfights are held each Sunday afternoon. There, in the empty arena, they practice bullfighting. Their "fierce bull" is a pair of horns mounted on a home-made wheelbarrow. One boy practices with a large cape while his friend wheels the dummy bull in charge after charge at the young "matador."

Miguel is determined to fight a real bull at the first opportunity. Why? For the same reason many boys in the United States dream of becoming a star in professional baseball or football. Instead of baseball heroes, the idols of Mexican boys are the great stars of bullfighting.

The Plaza México, where teenagers practice with the bull-on-wheels, can hold 50,000 people. Each

18

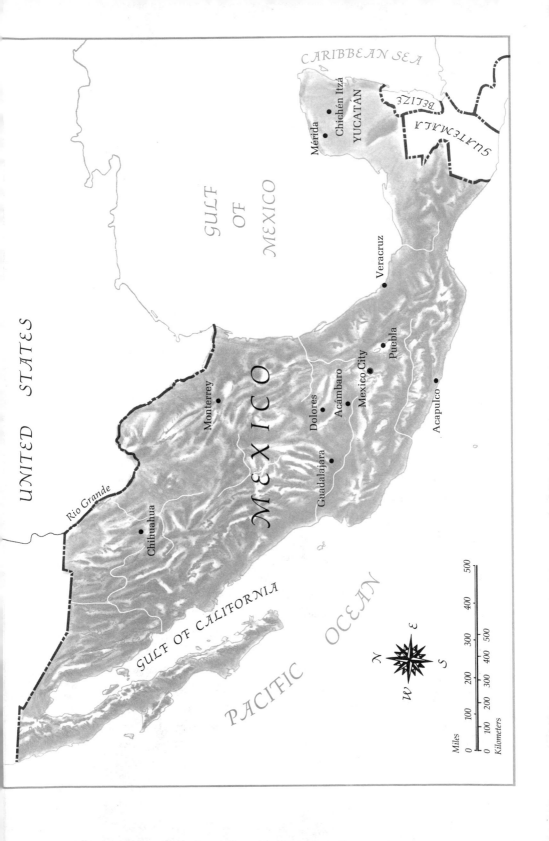

Sunday afternoon during the bullfight season, from November through February, the huge arena is packed with bullfight fans.

They watch an experienced matador who can cause the bull to charge within inches of his body. When he does this with a graceful swirl of his cape, the crowd shouts a thunderous *"Olé!"** — meaning "Well done!"

The Mexican people inherited bullfighting from Spain, along with their language. Bullfights are held in several countries of Latin America. Spectators consider a bullfight not as a sport but as a moving spectacle. In this living drama, the savage bull represents death; the fighter in his gold costume, life. The object is for life to dispose of death as gracefully as possible after defying its dangers.

Miguel's sister, María,* doesn't take her brother's ambition to be a bullfighter seriously. But one big difference between her and many girls in the United States is that she would never laugh at him about his wild dreams — even if she became quite angry at him. She'd be much more likely to tease him about his girl friend.

Mexican women, like women throughout much of Latin America, have traditionally taken a back seat to men. But this situation is changing, especially among the country's growing middle class. More and more city girls such as María are no longer satisfied to play a meek, submissive role around the house.

Still, some changes come slowly. María's family is strict, and she won't be allowed on an unsupervised date until she's at least 18.

The new and the old clash in Mexico — just as they do in the United States. But in countries like Mexico, the new doesn't always win. Tradition is still very strong in Mexico.

Chapter 2

City and Country

ON THEIR WAY to school each day, Miguel and María pass through the streets of a city rebuilding itself. In September 1985, a series of earthquakes devastated Mexico City. The disaster killed more than 7,000 people and did $5 billion worth of damage. Hundreds of buildings collapsed, including many of the capital's sleekest towers of steel and glass.

Still standing are some of the oldest buildings in the Western hemisphere. A 400-year-old stone cathedral in Mexico city is the largest in Latin America. It was constructed by the Spanish *conquistadores**—conquerors—of Mexico. They built it on the foundations of another temple built earlier by Indians who had been living in Mexico for centuries when the Spanish arrived. For Mexicans, such buildings are constant reminders of their rich Indian and Spanish heritage.

Mexico City's Paseo de la Reforma* is one of the broadest and most beautiful avenues in the world. It too was designed by the Spaniards hundreds of years

21

*In Mexico City streets, 400-year-old churches
built by the conquistadores are mingled
back-to-back with the shape of things to come.*

ago. Yet it is wide enough to accommodate more traffic than many streets in newer cities — and still has room for proud statues, grassy malls, and splashing water fountains.

Downtown Mexico City never seems to sleep. Crowds stroll until long after midnight along the brightly lit streets. Whatever the hour, the people seldom seem in a hurry.

Many Latin Americans are on a different timetable from people in the United States. Their work day is cut by a *siesta*. This is a midday break which allows workers to have a long lunch and perhaps a little nap.

22

The shops make up for this lost time by remaining open at night, long after most stores in the United States have closed. With a large lunch and an hour's sleep behind them, many Latin Americans aren't ready for the evening meal — or to go to bed — until late.

The daily routine of Mexico City's millions of people is hardly ever interrupted by extremes of weather. This old city is in the tropics and, ordinarily, would be a hot place to live. But since it is located on a plain nearly a mile and a half above sea level, it enjoys balmy temperatures almost the year round. It seldom gets hotter than 70 degrees in July, and seldom colder than 50 degrees in December. Once in a while snow falls on the city.

But for many who live in Mexico — as well as elsewhere in Latin America — life is not as easy-going as this ideal climate would suggest. Even in modern, bustling Mexico City many jobless people go hungry. In the country, lack of equipment, droughts, and poor soil keep many farmers very poor.

When Miguel and María visit their grandparents in the village of Acámbaro,* they don't sleep on a regular bed. Instead, they spend the night on a makeshift bed of bamboo sticks placed on two sawhorses. The grandparents themselves prefer to sleep on the floor. They claim it's more comfortable.

Acámbaro is like many villages throughout Latin America. Many of its residents prefer the old ways of doing things. Only recently did the grandparents fit their house with electricity and running water. Before that, they lighted the house with kerosene lamps and hauled water in buckets from a nearby fountain.

Now things have changed in the village. Indeed, they have probably changed more in the past 20 years than they did in the previous 400. Despite the con-

23

venience of electricity and running water, Miguel's grandparents aren't sure the changes are all that good. They like doing things the old ways and find it difficult to adjust to the new.

For example, the grandmother still does her laundry in a nearby stream, even though she has running water in the house. Why does she still do it in the stream? That's the way women in her village have always done the laundry, she says. Besides, how will she gossip with the women of the village if she must sit in her house doing the washing?

Early each morning, Miguel's grandmother uses corn meal to make *tortillas**, the daily bread of the Mexican people. Villagers who can afford it now buy their tortillas, already made, in the local marketplace. White bread and other American-style foods are viewed as symbols of prosperity and progress.

Tortillas are made by mixing a batter of corn meal and slapping the cake into shape between the flats of the hands. Walking along the village's narrow streets in early morning, a visitor can hear the cheery clapping noise of women making tortillas inside the thin-walled houses.

The corn which Miguel helps harvest can make the difference between whether his grandparents will be adequately fed during the winter or whether they will sometimes go hungry. Even good harvest years are seldom good enough to let the old folks save a little money. So they have nothing to tide them over the poor seasons unless their family helps them out.

Because they receive help from their children and grandchildren, Miguel's grandparents never have to skip a meal. But there are millions of Latin Americans who do.

Life is made a little less grim to the people of Latin America by the many festivals and other celebrations.

24

Sometimes a man can be as slow to change old ways as oxen are to plow a furrow. This farmer uses wooden plow because he fears steel will "freeze" the soil and damage crops.

For, rich or poor, Latin Americans have one thing in common. Most of them are filled with a zest for life. If there's anything to celebrate, they'll celebrate it.

There are many occasions for *fiestas**, even in villages such as Acámbaro. There are religious holidays that are celebrated throughout most of Latin America, such as Ash Wednesday, Holy Week, and Christmas. There are strictly local fiestas, too. Acámbaro, for instance, celebrates 53 festivals every year. Some last as long as three or four days. But not everyone has enough

25

It's fiesta day, and these charros, *Mexican cowboys, are out for fun. They're about to enter a "ribbon race" in which they'll try to spear rings hanging from ribbons.*

time to attend every fiesta.

A fiesta usually consists of a big fair in the center of town. The people stroll among the booths, buying candy, sodas, and fancy tortillas while awaiting the exciting main events.

One is a horse race by *charros*,* Mexican cowboys. It is called the "ribbon race." Girls of the village donate colored ribbons which are hung from a wire stretched across the road. From each ribbon dangles a ring. The object of the race is for the charro, riding at

26

top speed beneath the wire, to spear one of the rings with a stick.

If a charro is able to spear a ring, he kneels before the girl who donated the ribbon. She gives him the ribbon as a keepsake. Also, if she is bold enough, she may give him a kiss.

Festivals also feature other rodeo events, dances, and parades. At night fireworks splash color in the sky. While all this is going on, many people go to church to pray. Most Mexicans are Roman Catholics, and most fiestas have religious meanings.

Some celebrations aren't big or noisy. On Miguel's 15th birthday, he awoke to the tune of "Las Mañanitas."* This traditional song for birthdays comes from the state of Jalisco but is sung in several versions all over Mexico. Miguel's father had put the song on the record player while his son was still asleep.

Music plays a big part in the life of Latin Americans. In small towns of Mexico, the serenade still is important in courtship. In the early evening, the young man stands outside the girl's window and plays her favorite songs upon a guitar. In larger cities, however, many young people have abandoned such old customs. Music for a serenade in Mexico City is likely to be furnished by a high-powered portable stereo.

Some old customs, by contrast, still remain strongly in evidence. Religion is very much a part of everyday Mexican life. Almost every home has a table decorated with statues of saints. Many buses, in addition to a religious medal hanging from the rear-view mirror, are apt to have a picture of the driver's patron saint pasted above the windshield. And most families don't consider a girl really married unless she has taken her vows in church. To provide for a big wedding, families often go deeply into debt.

Chapter 3

The Conquerors

TODAY'S MEXICO has many reminders of its ancient past. Outside of Mexico City are great stone pyramids that rival those of the ancient Egyptians. These were built by the Aztecs, who ruled during the 1400's and early 1500's. The Aztecs built their great pyramid atop the ruins of another, much older pyramid. And beneath the ruins of that pyramid is the rubble of still another pyramid, much older than the two above it. The people who built this bottom structure are one of the many mysteries of Mexican history.

Not all the Indian peoples of ancient Mexico lived in the country's central region near what is now Mexico City. One of the oldest—and most mysterious—of these peoples were the Mayans*. About 2,500 years ago, the Mayans had their original home far to the south in the highlands of what is now Guatemala. For some unknown reason, most of the Mayans moved to the hot, parched Yucatán* peninsula of Mexico, which separates the Gulf of Mexico from the Caribbean Sea.

Rosa lives in Mérida,* the largest city in the Yucatán. She is 12 and has always lived in Mérida. Her parents also have lived all their lives in Mérida and so have her grandparents and her great-grandparents. That's as far back as the family can trace their ancestry, but if they could go back further, they would probably find that their ancestors have been in the Mérida area for more than 2,000 years.

Rosa does not yet know what she is going to do with her life, but she may be the first member of her family to leave Mérida. The Yucatán used to be the most remote section of Mexico. It wasn't until almost 1960 that a highway was built to connect it with the rest of the country. But whether she leaves or not, Rosa does not want to forget her Mayan heritage entirely.

She knows that the ancient Mayans were interested in mathematics and were expert astronomers. They devised a 365-day calendar that was more accurate than the calendar used by Europeans at the time Mexico was conquered. The Mayan year was divided into 18 months of 20 days each, plus an extra month of five days. Using this calendar, the Mayans could predict the dates of eclipses and the arrival of comets.

The Mayans worked out sundials and built temples for the worship of their gods. They decorated their buildings with stone sculptures, carvings, and murals. They also had a written language. It was made up of 850 pictures instead of letters. Samples of it still exist today, but the trouble is that experts can understand only a little bit of it.

The Aztecs were less gifted as astronomers than the Mayans. But the Aztecs built probably the most powerful nation in all of North America before the arrival of white men from Europe.

Many centuries ago Mayan priests devised a system of picture-writing which has stumped the experts to this day. These experts believe that dots and dashes represent numbers and figures represent ideas. They've deciphered enough of the writing to know that it accurately predicts the dates of certain eclipses. But they've never been able to read all of the three Mayan books still in existence. The art work (left) comes from one of these books. Do you have any idea what it may mean?

At their height the Aztecs ruled most of central and southern Mexico and some of Central America. They developed a form of writing. Aztec agents kept the capital informed of goings-on throughout the empire by hand-delivered written messages. The Aztec people built many of the pyramids Miguel sees, wove cloth, and made jewelry and carvings of gold and precious stones. The Aztecs had another sure mark of civilization: taxes. But the Aztecs were, above all, warriors, and it was their warlike, and even blood-thirsty, habits that proved their undoing.

The Aztecs correctly believed that all life on Earth depends on the sun. But this belief took a terrifying turn. They believed that to be reborn and fight each day, the sun god and their other deities needed much nourishment. To the Aztecs, it meant the most precious food of all—human sacrifice. The Aztecs sacrificed prisoners by the tens of thousands.

One particular belief spurred the Aztecs to continue fighting with other Indians and to offer religions sacrifices to the gods. The Aztecs believed that they were a special people and that their ruler had been chosen by the gods to rule the world.

The Aztecs' days began to be numbered in the year 1519. One day Indian messengers brought back reports to the capital of strange, huge ships in the Gulf of Mexico.

Soon the empire of the Aztecs was throbbing with terrifying rumors. Among the deities worshipped by the Aztecs was Quetzalcoatl,* the white god. Hearing that light-skinned strangers had appeared aboard these ships, the Aztec people believed that Quetzalcoatl had returned to earth.

The leader of those aboard the ships was the Spanish *conquistador,* Hernán Cortés.* Cortés had a small force, only about 500 men. In Mexico there were about two million Indians. But Cortés had powerful weapons on his side. One weapon was gunpowder.

Though the Indians knew much about some things, they had never heard of firearms. They had also never seen a horse. Cortés' men were lightly armed by modern standards, but they were armed enough to conquer the awed and ill-armed Indians.

The bloodthirsty and aggressive ways of the Aztecs had made them many enemies among their Indian neighbors. Many of these decided to join Cortés on his march of conquest. Accompanied by a thousand of these new allies, Cortés and his men entered the great Aztec city of Tenochtitlán.* Moctezuma,* ruler of the Aztecs, received Cortés with honor. It is not clear whether or not Moctezuma believed Cortés was the returning white god, Quetzalcoatl, but many of his subjects certainly believed it.

Moctezuma tried to bribe Cortés to leave Mexico with treasure chests of gold, silver, jade, and other valuables. It was the wrong thing to do, for Cortés and his men were only more determined to conquer the Aztecs when they saw the wealth awaiting them. Cortés decided that the only way to conquer the Aztecs was by seizing Moctezuma and holding him captive.

He soon found a good excuse to do so. He received word that a garrison of men he had left on the coast had been attacked by Indians. In retaliation Cortés and his officers put Moctezuma in chains.

The Spanish conquerors soon proved that they could be as cruel as the Indians they had defeated. After Cortés' men had put down the uprising on the coast, they burned the Indian leader of that attack at the stake.

Cortés then used a psychological weapon. With his own hands, he unlocked the irons from Moctezuma,

THE APPROACH OF THE EMPEROR.

In the 1500's the Aztec empire went in a few years
from fabulous splendor to complete collapse. Top,
elaborately dressed Aztec warriors bow to their
emperor. Drawing (below), done by an Indian of the
time, depicts another tribe carrying supplies for the
Spanish attacking the Aztecs. Not all Indians did so
willingly, however, as scene at bottom right indicates.

chalchicueyeca

freeing the Aztec ruler. From then on, Moctezuma — grateful and vastly relieved — was Cortés' supporter. But the Aztecs soon revolted against the rule of the Spanish. When Moctezuma tried to tell his people to put down their arms, he was stoned to death.

The revolt was put down, and the Spanish destroyed the whole of the city of Tenochtitlán with its palaces, storehouses, and canals. Upon the rubble of Tenochtitlán, the Spanish built a new city, later named Mexico City.

Many Indians of Latin America, after first fighting the Europeans invaders, began living beside them in peace. Unlike many early settlers of North America, few of the Spaniards brought wives and daughters to the New World. They had come to explore, conquer, and seek riches, not to settle down. But those who stayed tended to take Indian women for their wives

Intermarriage between the Spanish explorers and Indian women soon became common. Today, most of the Mexican people are *mestizos**, of mixed Indian and Spanish ancestry.

Miguel's and María's grandparents still speak the traditional Indian language in addition to speaking Spanish. Several of the older villagers don't speak Spanish at all.

In many places of Latin America, the Indians remain even more isolated from modern culture. They speak their own language, follow ancient customs, and remain ignorant of the outside world. No one Indian language is understood by all Indians. It's estimated that there are from 50 to 100 Indian languages spoken in various parts of Mexico alone.

This tremendous diversity of language is one of Mexico's main distinctions as a nation. It's also a reason why the Mexican government has sometimes found it difficult to unite its people.

Double-check

Review

1. What is the language of Mexico and of most other countries of Latin America?

2. In a bullfight, what do the bull and the fighter represent?

3. What is a *siesta?*

4. Who were the Mayans?

5. Who was Moctezuma?

Discussion

1. These chapters discuss some ways in which land and climate affect the lives of people in Mexico and other parts of Latin America. *Where* people live often influences *how* they live. Think of ways this is true for your community. Then compare your community with the information about Latin America. Would it make sense to say, "Geography is destiny"?

2. Chapter 2 points out, "Many Latin Americans are on a different timetable from people in the United States." Meals are eaten much later, shops stay open past midnight, and evening events begin at 10 P.M. instead of at 8 P.M. as they do in the U.S. Would you enjoy such a pattern of life? Will such a timetable ever develop in the United States? Why, or why not?

3. Miguel's grandparents and rural citizens of Mexico and other Latin American countries have resisted many changes in their traditional ways of life and languages. What, if anything, could or should their governments do about this? Give reasons for your answers.

Activities

1. Some students might prepare a large wall map of Latin America for use with these and future chapters. They could use the map on page 6 as a guide and then add information to it from other maps, including others in this book.

2. Five words in Chapter 1 are starred (*). This indicates that they are in the Pronunciation Guide. A committee of students might assume primary responsibility for teaching fellow students how to pronounce these words. They could then do this, in advance, for all future chapters.

3. The photo essays near the center of this book contain several photos showing the diversity of land, people, economy, and culture in Latin America. You might look at these photos now, and then mark on a map the places they show.

Skills

MEXICAN ALIENS DEPORTED FROM THE U.S.

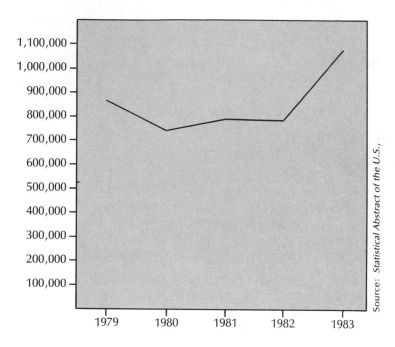

Source: *Statistical Abstract of the U.S.,*

Use the line graph above and information in Chapters 1 through 3 to answer the following questions.

1. What do the numbers to the left of the graph represent?
   (a) Mexicans who were in the U.S. illegally and sent back.
   (b) Aliens from the U.S. who were in Mexico illegally and sent back.
   (c) The Mexican population.

2. What is the source of information in this graph?
   (a) Mexican census figures.
   (b) *Statistical Abstract of the U.S.*
   (c) Chapter 3

3. How many Mexican aliens were deported from the U.S. in 1979?
   (a) not given   (b) 866,800   (c) 795,400

4. During what year did the U.S. deport the fewest number of Mexican aliens?
   (a) 1980   (b) 1982   (c) 1983

5. What does a quick glance at this graph tell you about the immigration policy of the United States?

Chapter 4

The Cry of Dolores

EACH DAY on the bus to school, Miguel and María pass Mexico's National Palace. This beautiful structure was originally built by Cortés. It now houses the nation's executive offices, but for hundreds of years it was the residence of Mexico's Spanish rulers.

Spain insisted that those who governed New Spain, as Mexico was called until the early 1800's, be born in Spain. Not only did the chief administrator, or *viceroy*, have to be born in Spain but all his major assistants had to be Spanish as well.

The ambition of many Spanish settlers was to obtain land of their own and to grow rich by having their fields worked by Indians. Some of these settlers received deeds to large tracts of property and the right to make Indians living on that property work for them.

It was also the landowners' task to make Christians of the Indians. The landowners held great power over the Indians, and many Indians quickly declared — in

✑ "Death to bad government! Death to the Spanish!"

public, at least — that they had been converted to the new faith. But many continued to practice their own religions in secret.

Despite Spain's heavy-handed rule, there was no serious rebellion as viceroy after viceroy — 62 in all — presided over New Spain. But in 1810 a parish priest in the village of Dolores* rang a bell and shouted a slogan which soon was on the lips of people throughout Mexico:

Long live our Lady of Guadalupe! Death to bad government! Death to the Spanish!

This parish priest was Father Miguel Hidalgo y Costilla.* Hidalgo's words became known as *El Grito de Dolores* (The Cry of Dolores), named for the village in which the revolution began.

Hidalgo mustered a force of armed men which soon took a number of towns. In January 1811, he was defeated in battle and taken prisoner. He and his fellow "troublemakers" were put to death by the Spanish. But Hidalgo had added to the fires of freedom now burning in Mexico, and the battle to rid Mexico of Spanish control went on.

Today Hidalgo is venerated as "the father of Mexican independence." Statues of Hidalgo adorn Mexican parks, and his profile appears on five-peso coins. The bell he rang to draw attention to his words is now known as Mexico's Independence Bell. It is enshrined near the National Palace. Each September 16 — the anniversary of the day Hidalgo began his revolution — the president of Mexico appears on the balcony of the National Palace and repeats *El Grito de Dolores*.

Hidalgo's slogan and the fighting that followed

didn't bring freedom to Mexico. Other uprisings followed Hidalgo's, but Spain managed to hold onto Mexico until 1821.

In that year, the Mexicans rose and drove out the Spanish, establishing a republic. The Spanish were gone, but a century of turmoil was just beginning. During this period, Mexico suffered under a string of weak presidents, punctuated by periods of rule by strong dictators. There were exceptions, of course, and one such exception was the 14 years from 1858 to 1872 when Benito Juarez,* a full-blooded Indian, was president of Mexico. Juarez helped unify his country, made many needed reforms, and led Mexican forces in repelling an invasion backed by the army of France. But Juarez died before his work was done, and Mexico fell back into its old ways after his death.

Miguel's grandfather was just a boy when the last of the dictators, Porfirio Díaz,* was overthrown. That revolution plunged Mexico into a period of conflict as bloody as the war for independence a century earlier. But out of it modern Mexico gradually emerged as a healthy democracy.

Chapter 5

The Mexican Revolution

PORFIRIO DÍAZ had been in power for 35 years when he was overthrown in 1911. Under Díaz, foreign money had poured into Mexico — but few Mexicans ever saw it. By 1910 almost all of Mexico's wealth was controlled by foreign bankers and financiers. Most of the land was owned by a few thousand wealthy families. The condition of Mexican peasants had not changed much since the days of Spanish rule.

In 1911 a number of rebellions broke out all over Mexico. The aging Díaz went into exile. For the next few years, the country was in an uproar as army fought army for control of Mexico. Governments came and went, alliances formed and dissolved, and even the U.S. was drawn in when one of the rebel chieftains, Pancho Villa,* raided a town across the border in New Mexico and killed 17 people there. A U.S. expedition under General John J. Pershing (who later achieved fame as commander of U.S. forces in

"Land! Land! Land!" became the battle cry between 1911 and 1917, when millions of landless peasants fought and died in the Mexican Revolution.

Europe during World War I) invaded Mexico in search of Villa, but never was able to catch him.

By 1917 things had quieted enough for prominent Mexicans to meet and draw up a constitution. It was the most revolutionary ever written in the New World. It became a model for many other Latin American constitutions. Land was to be given to the people. The rights of workers to strike were spelled out. Social security was to be put into effect — 15 years before such a plan began to catch on in the United States. The powers of the church were defined and limited.

In the 1930's and '40's, the aims of the Mexican Revolution were put into full effect — a quarter of a century after they had become slogans. Millions of acres of land were given to peasants. As a result, Miguel's grandfather was given the use of about two acres of land.

During World War II, Mexico proved that it had come of age as a country. It was the only Latin American nation, except for Brazil, to take an active part in fighting for the free world. The postwar nation continued to build up its economy. The power of the army in politics declined, and revolution seemed a thing of the past.

Today, one of Mexico's greatest strengths is its stable, democratic government. Presidential elections are held every six years, and Mexico's presidents cannot serve more than one term in office. The Institutional Revolutionary Party (PRI) has governed the nation since 1929 and is a coalition of many groups—labor unions, peasants, government workers, the military, and the middle class. The PRI's power makes Mexico a one-party state. Although corruption is a continuing problem and much poverty remains, most Mexicans continue to support the PRI's record of better housing, food distribution, and education.

Chapter 6

Pesos and Poverty

MANY U.S. CITIZENS find it hard to understand Mexico. Mexico is their next-door neighbor, but so much about it seems different from the U.S. One of the big differences is poverty.

Compared to the U.S., Mexico suffers from more than its share of poverty. According to unofficial estimates by top Mexican economists, personal income averaged $23 a month in 1985. About 60 percent of the population struggles by on an income of about $3.66 a day—the minimum wage in Mexico City. At the top of the income ladder, about 10 percent of all Mexicans have incomes of $12,000 a year or higher.

Mexicans are touchy about poverty in their nation. They point out, correctly, that Mexico's standard of living is higher than that of most other nations in Latin America. For example, land ownership is distributed more fairly in Mexico than it is throughout much of the region. And Mexico has made great strides over the past 20 years. Three out of four Mexican homes now

*Behind Mexico's efforts to educate its young
people lies a struggle against poverty,
disease, and despair — a struggle often waged
in a humble, one-room schoolhouse.*

have electricity. Nearly nine out of ten Mexicans can now read.

Still, Mexico's leaders admit that their nation has much more to do in improving the lives of most of its citizens. Experts say that most Mexicans who are born poor have few opportunities for advancement. One problem is schooling. Mexico's constitution of 1917 declares that elementary education is to be free and compulsory. Yet now, 70 years later, some of the nation's school-age children have no schools to attend. Other's can't attend the schools that do exist. They are needed at home, on the farm, or on the job to help their families survive financially. Only one third of Mexico's school children finish the sixth grade. Only one fourth finish high school.

The few young people who graduated from college make up most of the elite of Mexico and other Latin American countries. They become the businessmen, the doctors, the lawyers, the college professors, and, often, the army officers. This extremely small upper class usually furnishes the political leaders who run the country.

Another reason Mexico is making slow progress in improving its people's lives is its fast-growing population. Since 1976, Mexico's population has soared from 58 million to nearly 80 million. More than half of Mexico's people are under 19. Each year, nearly one million young Mexicans enter the job market. Unfortunately, there isn't enough work to go around. Many of the young people are likely to go long periods without getting a job. About half of those who do get jobs are likely to be underemployed. That is, they hold part-time or low-paying jobs far beneath their abilities.

In rural areas, there is not enough farmland to go around. The younger children of farmers have little chance to make a living in rural areas. So, each day,

◄§ Despite its natural wealth and industrial strength, Mexico's economy is in deep trouble. The nation owes nearly $100 billion to foreign banks.

thousands of people leave Mexico's villages. Some head for the U.S. border with hopes of crossing over to find work there. Many others stream into Mexico's cities—especially Mexico City.

Today, Mexico City is the world's fastest-growing metropolis, bursting with 17 million people. And experts predict that, by the year 2000, Mexico City will become the world's largest city with 30 million residents. The government has built many low-cost housing projects. But new families keep coming to Mexico City faster than homes can be constructed for them. Six million city residents live in the shantytowns on the city's outskirts. Most of these people are squatters, living in shacks they built on someone else's land.

In all this poverty, however, there is pride—pride, for one thing, in a beautiful country. One of Mexico's richest natural resources is its beauty. Million of tourists each year come to see its natural wonders and colorful way of life. Most of these visitors are from the United States.

They lounge on the white beaches along Mexico's coasts. They marvel at snow-capped extinct volcanoes soaring majestically upward. Or they visit sparkling lakes where fishermen still fish with nets shaped like butterflies that were being used before the time of Cortés.

Wherever they go, they spend tourist dollars that help Mexico's economy. To attract tourists, Mexicans have built new highways, airports, and luxury resorts.

But the tourist trade doesn't seem to be the answer to Mexico's problems. Since the days of the Aztecs, this rich country hasn't learned to make the best use of its wealth for most of its people. Mexico is one of the world's leading producers of coffee, cotton, oranges, and sugar cane. It is also the world's leading silver producer. And it has large deposits of copper, oil, gold, and sulfur.

The biggest change in Mexico's economy over the past 40 years has been the growth of manufacturing. Factories produce everything from steel and cars to chemicals and electrical appliances. The Mexican economy is one of the most industrialized in Latin America.

Despite its natural wealth and industrial strength, Mexico's economy is in deep trouble. The nation owes nearly $100 billion to foreign banks. The reason, experts say, is bad planning and overspending.

In 1976, geologists discovered enormous oil and natural gas reserves in the Gulf of Mexico. PEMEX, the government-owned oil company, quickly hooked up its pumps to the new fields. When oil prices rose, Mexico cashed in.

Mexico's government borrowed vast sums of money to finance new development. Then, in the early 1980's, the price of oil plunged. Interest rates—the cost of borrowing—rose. Higher interest rates added to Mexico's huge debts. Economic growth slowed.

To find the money to pay back the banks, the government was forced to slash spending on everything from health care programs to plans for new schools. It also cut subsidies for many foods. Many workers lost their jobs or had their wages reduced.

Today, the Mexican government is struggling to repair the economy and control the nation's birth rate to improve the quality of life for its citizens.

Double-check

Review

1. What was the ambition of many Spanish settlers?

2. Who is venerated as "the father of Mexican independence"?

3. By 1910 almost all of Mexico's wealth was controlled by whom?

4. What is the daily wage that about 60 percent of all Mexicans earn?

5. What is one reason Mexico is making little progress in improving the lives of its citizens?

Discussion

1. Do you think it was fair for the Spanish settlers to force the Indians living on their property to work for them? How might this arrangement have harmed Mexico — then and now?

2. How could, or should, a society (with or without government involvement) balance the need of children for education with the need of their families to have the children work? Who should make these decisions? How much education should be the *minimum* requirement? At what age should children be allowed to work? Give reasons for your answers.

3. In the early 1900's, foreign investors owned most Mexican land and companies. This was changed by the revolution. But now the situation is similar in regard to many Mexican companies and mines. What, if anything, should the Mexican government do about this? For years U.S. companies have owned controlling interests in businesses all over the world. Now many foreign investors are buying control of companies and land in the U.S. What do you think about this?

Activities

1. A committee of students might prepare a bulletin board display and/or oral reports on aspects of life in Mexico, including art, music, architecture, language, religion, dress, crafts, customs, politics, and the economy.

2. A Mexican immigrant to the U.S., or someone who has recently visited Mexico, might be invited to speak to the class. Students could prepare a list of questions for the speaker beforehand.

3. In 1980 the U.S. government estimated that there were three to six million Mexican immigrants living illegally in the U.S. Some students might research and report to the rest of the class on what is being done about illegal Mexican immigration into the U.S.

Skills

SCHOOL ENROLLMENT IN MEXICO

Level of School	Students (in thousands)			Teachers (in thousands)		
	1970	1975	1983	1970	1976	1983
Primary	9,248	12,148	15,222	201	256	415
Secondary	1,584	3,241	5,715	109	193	317
Higher	248	539	1,013	(NA)	41	86

Source: *Statistical Abstract of the U.S.,*
Britannica World Data

NA = Not Available

Use the table above and information in Chapters 4 through 6 to answer the following questions:

1. What do the numbers under the years represent?
(a) schools in Mexico
(b) students and teachers in Mexico
(c) children in Mexico

2. What does NA stand for?
(a) North America   (b) Not Available   (c) New Edition

3. How many secondary school teachers were there in 1983?
(a) 317   (b) 86   (c) 317,000

4. During what year was there the greatest number of college students?
(a) 1970   (b) 1976   (c) 1983

5. At which level of Mexican schools has the number of teachers almost tripled?
(a) primary   (b) secondary   (c) higher

2
BRAZIL

Chapter 7

Big Booming Brazil

MARCIA, LIKE María in Mexico City, is a Latin American girl. But there are many differences between them. For one, Marcia and María wouldn't be able to understand each other. María speaks Spanish. Marcia, who lives in Brazil, speaks Portuguese.

Another difference can be seen in their backgrounds and family histories. Maria's ancestry is Indian. Marcia's is both Portuguese and African.

Many millions of Brazilians have much the same ancestry as Marcia. Brazil, a big country on the move, is one of the world's most successful melting pots, and blacks have made a big contribution to its growth and success. So have the Indians.

Brazilians scoff at the racial troubles of other countries. They point with pride to the general lack of racial discrimination in their country where intermarriage among the races has long been commonplace.

Many of Brazil's most successful people have come from mixed racial backgrounds such as Marcia's. So, it's unlikely that Marcia will face racial discrimination as she pursues her ambition to become an artist.

If Marcia is to succeed as an artist, however, she will have to work hard just to find time to perfect her painting. For right now, she's having difficulty finishing high school. It isn't that she's poor in her studies. But Marcia's family is a large one. She has two sisters and five brothers. Each one must help add to the family income.

Only 15, Marcia works full-time as a typist and errand girl for a travel agency. She goes to high school at night, from 7:30 p.m. until 11. With such a busy schedule, she's usually hungry when the family has its main meal at about 6:30 p.m.

Marcia's father works for the water department. Yet, only a few years ago did her family's house receive running water. Even in large Latin American cities such as São Paulo*, many families must rely on wells.

Marcia's home has no telephone, but it does have a TV, and the family owns five radios. Mostly, though, Marcia reads avidly. She seldom has enough free time to go to the movies. And, even working so hard, she doesn't know how she'll ever get enough money to go to college. But meanwhile, she works—and dreams of her career as an artist.

Sao Paulo, the city in which Marcia lives, is one of the fastest-growing cities in the world. Its population is 26 times larger than it was in 1900. Today, with more than 14 million people, it already ranks as the fifth largest city in the world.

São Paulo is hundreds of years old. Brasilia,* the capital of Brazil, is brand new. It was carved from a desolate wilderness, in the late 1950's.

Brasilia's builders hoped the new city would solve

52

VENEZUELA

SURINAM

FR GUIANA

GUYANA

ATLANTIC OCEAN

EQUATOR

COLOMBIA

Amazon

Manaus •

Amazon

A M A Z O N I A N   R A I N   F O R E S T

• Belém

São Luís •

• Fortaleza

PERU

B R A Z I L

Natal •

São Francisco

Recife •

BOLIVIA

• Salvador

Brasilia •

MINAS
GERAIS

Campo Grande •

Belo Horizonte •

Paraná

Volta Redonda •

PARAGUAY

São Paulo •

Rio de Janeiro •

Santos •

ARGENTINA

RIO
GRANDE
DO SUL

N

W   E

S

PACIFIC OCEAN

Pôrto Alegre •

Miles
0   100   200   300   400   500

URUGUAY

0   100 200 300 400 500
Kilometers

◆§ Everybody in Brazil wanted to live along the Atlantic Coast.

one of Brazil's oldest problems. The problem was that almost everybody in Brazil wanted to live along the Atlantic coast. That was where the jobs, the businesses, the industries were.

This biggest country of Latin America has about 139 million people, nearly half the population of all South America. But many of them, about 60 percent, are crowded together in the big coastal cities.

The interior of the country, meanwhile, is vast — and almost empty. Millions of square miles are sparsely settled and largely undeveloped. This land, two thirds of Brazil's total area, is home to less than 10 per cent of the nation's people.

Brasilia is known as the world's first air-age capital. The whole country of Brazil has fewer paved roads than many states in the U.S. The only practical way of reaching this most modern of capitals is to fly there since it is far from the other main cities. Symbolically, the city was laid out in the shape of a huge airplane.

Brasilia was officially declared the capital in 1960, and the seat of government was gradually transferred from the old capital, Rio de Janeiro,* 600 miles to the southeast.

Brasilia was planned to the last detail. Its planners solved many traffic problems long before there was traffic. All of its streets are one way. No traffic signals stop motorists zipping along major traffic arteries.

Brasilia is not only new; it's beautiful. Its public buildings are sleek and modern. Its squares are graced by massive sculptures (see photo essay, page 84).

In many respects, Brasilia is a "dream city." But at first it didn't strike most people as their idea of a

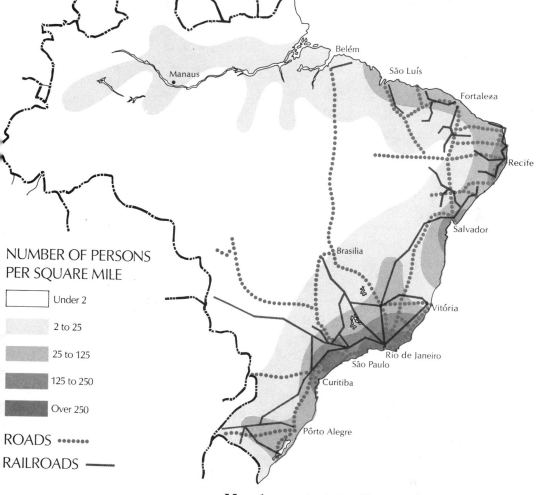

NUMBER OF PERSONS
PER SQUARE MILE

☐ Under 2

2 to 25

25 to 125

125 to 250

Over 250

ROADS ••••••

RAILROADS ——

Map shows extent of settlement near Brazil's coast and lack of settlement in the vast interior.

place to live. Their chief objection was that the new city was in the middle of nowhere. To encourage people to move to Brasilia, the government offered its government workers fine apartments at low rents. They were also offered free bus service to their offices and, for their children, good schools and playgrounds.

People from the coastal areas are gradually moving inland to Brasilia. The government continues to provide extra benefits to keep its workers in Brasilia happy. Whether the new city will benefit the country's development as much, or as soon, as planned can't yet be answered. But the city is growing fast.

55

Chapter 8

Growing Pains

BRAZIL COVERS 3,286,473 square miles — larger than the continental U.S. It is the fifth largest country in the world and its frontiers touch every country of South America except Chile and Ecuador. It has vast mineral and agricultural resources, many of them hardly tapped.

The state of Minas Gerais* ("general mines") alone contains nearly one fourth of the world's known iron ore reserves. Brazil is the world's largest coffee producer. The region around São Paulo also produces sugar cane, cotton, oranges, and cattle.

But much of Brazil is virtually uninhabited. One unpeopled area consists of the vast rain forest of the Amazon River. Though hundreds of thousands of people, mainly Indians, scratch out a living in this region, the basin is so vast that its population averages about one person to every square mile.

In this rain forest (the world's largest), enormous trees have high boughs so thickly interlaced that they completely blot out the sky. A traveler could go hundreds of miles through this forest and seldom see the sun. Above him would always be the dense canopy of green leaves.

There are no seasons in this forest, located near the Equator. Rainfall is always plentiful, so the leaves never change color.

More water flows in the Amazon River and its tributaries than in any other river in the world. During the rainy season, from November to June, it discharges more than seven million cubic feet of water *every second*. That's almost 14 times the amount of water that drains from the largest U.S. river, the Mississippi.

The Amazon basin hold the world's greatest diversity of plants and animals. In one square mile, scientists have found more than 3,000 species—insects that eat birds, vines that strangle trees, colonies of monkeys.

But the Amazon and other Latin American rain forests are threatened by the mass migration of people. Thousands of families from city slums and poor mountain regions are moving into these fragile jungle areas.

Only two percent of the Amazon basin has soil rich enough for farming. Newcomers who try to farm take all the nutrients from the land within a few seasons. Then they abandon the barren land and begin somewhere else. In this way, settlers are clearing a million trees a day and destroying an area the size of Pennsylvania every year. Experts say that in 20 years much of Latin America's rain forests could be gone.

João's* world is the swampland of the Amazon. He lives in a little town built on many islands. The only way to get around is by boat. The nearest city, Belém, is a seven-hour boat trip away.

"I was born on our island, and so were my mother and father," João says. "And his father before him was a farmer on this same island."

João's father owns 224 rubber trees, which grow

naturally on his small "plantation." João helps his father collect the milky juice in buckets. When the juice hardens, it becomes crude rubber, which the family sells.

Their house is of wood and has a thatched roof. Its four rooms have little furniture. Cooking is done in a box lined with clay. The family sleeps in hammocks, taken down during the day.

João is 13 years old. He's still in the third grade. It's doubtful that he'll go much farther.

"We don't have any school in town," he explains. "Two years ago, when I was 11, I started school at a town on the other side of the Amazon. But it was too much trouble getting across the river twice a day, so I quit and went back to work on Father's plantation.

"Last year I had a chance to go into the second grade at a town 60 miles away. I stayed at my brother's home. School was held in the teacher's house, from 4 to 6:30 p.m. We weren't allowed to take the books out of school. There were 30 pupils studying reading and writing. I haven't learned a lot of the things I would like to know."

Many American boys João's age might even envy him for his almost Robinson Crusoe existence. "Sometimes I take Father's gun and go hunting wild pigs, which we call *porca*," he says. "Parrots are good eating, too."

It seems certain that João will spend the rest of his days in a shack on the river just as his father and grandfather have before him. Life is lived in set patterns in Amazonia, and few people alter the pattern.

Amazonia is also the home of Brazil's primitive Indians. It's estimated that 800,000 of them live in northern Brazil's jungles the way their forefathers did centuries ago.

Most of these Indians do not understand Portu-

*Serene and splendid, the Amazon River
serves as the major nerve center for Amazonia,
a dense tropical wilderness of towering trees,
wild animals, and primitive Indian peoples.*

guese, and many tribes cannot understand one another. Some of the tribes still hold to strange and sometimes cruel customs. In one tribe, no family has more than three children. If a fourth is born, it is killed at birth.

Most of Brazil's Indians live in such remote regions that no one is sure just how many there are. Several things make it difficult to turn these Indians into practicing citizens of a modern country. One is their hostility to outside influence. Another is that they often seem physically "allergic" to the white man. Many Indians, for example, apparently have no natural immunity to the common cold. A single white man suffering from a cold can spread it throughout a whole Indian village. Indians often die from this white man's malady.

☆   ☆   ☆   ☆   ☆   ☆   ☆   ☆   ☆

Brazilians may not be the most carefree people in the world. But sometimes they act as though they are — especially at *Carnaval** time. In the four days before Ash Wednesday everyone celebrates, rich and poor alike.

Virtually all Brazilian cities celebrate Carnaval, but the wildest is Rio de Janeiro. During this spree, hard-working students try to forget such unpleasant facts of life as that Rio universities are forced to turn away two out of three qualified applicants. Women in the *favelas,** the shantytowns on the hillsides, try to forget that food is scarce and spend their few coins on bright costume materials. The Brazil that gave the world such happy rhythms as the *samba* and *bossa nova* soon is in full sway.

Carnaval is more than just celebration. It also involves many of the beliefs retained from worship of African deities. Voodoo, for example, is still practiced among many of the poorer descendants of African slaves.

João is by no means the only Brazilian student whose education is being neglected. Brazilian law says that children must attend school until they're at least 14. But only schools in large cities have enough teachers and classrooms for the law to be enforced. As in most of Latin America, in remote districts only the children of wealthier parents are assured of a decent schooling.

As a result, only about three fourths of all Brazilians are able to read and write. Opportunities for education are improving. This is especially true in the urban areas. Still, many young Brazilians are not attending any kind of school.

The favelas that overlook Rio de Janeiro have been described as among the worst slums in the world. But Severino,* who lives in a favela, doesn't think of his neighborhood as a slum. To Severino, it's just the place where he has always lived. And he doesn't think it's such a bad place. Living high on a hillside gives him an eagle's eye view of the graceful arc of the Copacabana beach and the elegant, expensive hotels that line it. Severino's family will never be able to afford a vacation. But he has only to take a bus down the hill and he can spend his days on the white sands of the Copacabana.

Most of the houses in Severino's neighborhood are one-room shacks made of slabs of wood. In other favelas they may be made of sheets of tin or even cardboard. In some cases, a family of eight or 10 must use their one room as bedroom, kitchen, and living room. Garbage is dumped out the window because there is no other place for it. Severino's family is lucky enough to live near an electricity line which they tap, "free of charge." They must, however, haul water uphill from a pump several hundred feet away.

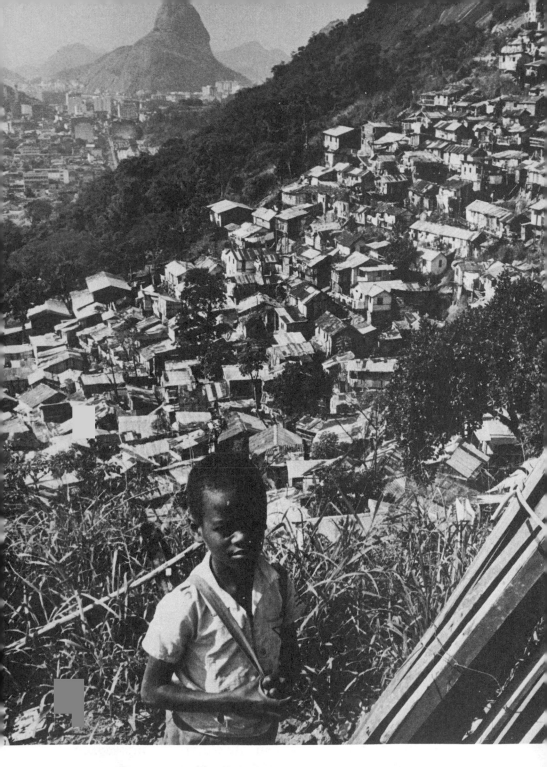

*Perched on hills of Rio de Janeiro are favelas,
slums, home to almost one million of Rio's poor.*

Even with some effort at building decent low-cost housing, Rio still has well over one million people living in its favelas. And that number is growing with each day. Why do people come there?

Most of the people of the favelas are recent immigrants from rural areas of Brazil where living conditions are even worse than they are in the slums. Many were drawn to Rio by the dream of high-paying jobs. When they arrived in the city, they found they had none of the skills required to do anything more than the most menial work. Others were bored with life in the farming country and wanted to be a part of the exciting life of Rio.

And who are these people who must live in the favelas? Despite Brazil's protests that racial discrimination doesn't exist in this country, the great majority of favela inhabitants are blacks.

Yet when Severino hears on his transistor radio of racial troubles in the U.S., he doesn't quite understand what all the fuss is about. The reason for this is there is little open racial discrimination in Brazil.

Brazilian-style discrimination is based not on race, but on social class — the prestige a person has from his job, his income, his friends, his manners, his education. But the blacker you are in Brazil, the more likely you are to find yourself near the bottom of the social ladder.

Black victims of this discrimination have one consolation, however small. The poor black man is on the same social footing as a poor white man. But if either of them tries to work his way up the social ladder in class-conscious Brazil, he's likely to run into great complications. His lack of education, his dress and mannerisms will be noticed — even if the color of his skin is ignored. No matter what his skin color, doors will be closed to him.

Double-check

Review

1. What was one of Brazil's oldest problems?

2. What did the Brazilian government offer its workers to encourage them to move to Brasilia?

3. How does Brazil compare in size to other nations of the world? How does its rain forest compare?

4. What are two reasons people of the *favelas* were drawn to Rio?

5. Brazilian-style discrimination is based not on race, but on what factor?

Discussion

1. Would you move to Brasilia if you lived along Brazil's coast? Why, or why not? Do you think many Brazilians will ever move into the interior? If they do, how will this affect the country's development?

2. Why do you think the Brazilian government wants to turn its primitive Indians into "practicing citizens of a modern country"? Do you think the Indians should be made to live in modern society? Or should the Indians be left alone to live as they choose in remote regions? Give the reasons for your answers.

3. In what ways are people discriminated against in the United States? How is this similar to, or different from, the ways people are discriminated against in Brazil? Do you think the reasons for and the results of all types of discrimination are the same? What aspects of Brazilian history might have led to the development of class discrimination? Will this ever change? Explain your answers.

Activities

1. A committee of students might prepare a bulletin board display and/or oral reports on aspects of life in Brazil, including art, music, architecture, language, religion, dress, crafts, customs, politics, and the economy.

2. Some students might write or draw advertisements to be published in Brazilian newspapers or magazines encouraging Brazilians to move to Brasilia. Other students could prepare radio or TV ads, which they could read aloud or act out for the rest of the class. Afterward the class could vote to choose the most effective ads.

3. Three students might role-play a conversation between Marcia, João, and Severino in which they talk about their lives and how they react to the possibility of changing places.

64

Skills

Use the maps on pages 53 and 55 and information in Chapters 7 and 8 to answer the following questions.

1. What body of water surrounds the northern and eastern shores of Brazil?

2. The Amazon River flows in what part of Brazil?

3. What do the dotted orange lines in the map on page 55 stand for?

4. How many people per square mile live in the area around Manaus?

5. The city in which Marcia lives is about how far from Brasilia?

Chapter 9

The Bubbling Pot

THE MIXING of races in Brazil began more than 400 years ago, shortly after Portugal began settling its new possession. But the destiny of Brazil was decided even before the Portuguese discovered the country.

In 1497-98 the Portuguese navigator, Vasco da Gama, found an all-water route to the Indies and Spice Islands by sailing around the Cape of Good Hope at the southern tip of Africa. This new route promised to bring Portugal a fortune in trade, and King Manuel I was eager to make use of it. Manuel sent another captain, Pedro Alvares Cabral,* with a large armada to duplicate Vasco da Gama's feat.

Off the Gulf of Guinea on Africa's west coast, the winds often die down, becalming any vessel in those waters. To avoid this, Cabral swung far to the west. On April 22, 1500, he unexpectedly sighted land.

The territory proved to be huge. But no precious metals were found, and Portugal's interest in its new land lagged for a quarter of a century. Rival countries such as France were quick to take advantage of Portugal's inattention. They began raiding the neglected territory, hauling away shiploads of a red wood used in making dyes. The name of the wood was *pau brasil*,* and the land itself — named after this wood — came to be known as Brazil.

Eventually, Portugal paid more attention to Brazil and began sending settlers. Some of them fathered children by Indian wives. These children were regarded as their fathers' rightful heirs and enjoyed full legal status. Already, Brazil's melting pot had begun to bubble.

Another race of people was thrown into that pot shortly after it was discovered that sugar could be raised on Brazilian plantations. Thousands of black slaves were brought from Africa to Brazil to work its sugar and cotton fields. Still more were put to work in Brazil's mines after gold was discovered in the late 1600's.

Portuguese cattlemen pushed inland, searching for new pasture for their herds. They were joined by missionaries, who traveled westward looking for Indians to convert to Christianity. And perhaps even more important were the *Bandeirantes** (flagbearers; called that because they bore the flag of the new colony). They were fortune-seekers on the prowl for Indian slaves, gold, and precious stones.

Brazil is the only colony in the New World which once served as the seat of government of its own European mother country. In 1807 the French leader Napoleon decided to invade Portugal. The Portuguese ruler, Dom João, believed it useless to fight. Instead, he sought refuge in Brazil and governed from there until 1821. When he returned to Portugal, he left Brazil in the hands of his son, Dom Pedro.

Portugal's ruling body, the Cortés, ordered Dom Pedro to return to Europe. But he decided to stay in Brazil. On September 7, 1822, he proclaimed Brazil's independence and was crowned emperor.

The United States was the first country to recognize the new Brazilian government. Opposed by a number of Brazilian political leaders, Dom Pedro soon abdicated (left the throne) in 1831 in favor of his son, Dom Pedro II — who at the time was only five years old. Pedro II ruled until 1889.

The greatest accomplishment of Pedro II's rule was the abolition of slavery in 1888 — about 25 years after Lincoln signed the Emancipation Proclamation in the United States. But in 1889 the wealthy former slave-owners forced Dom Pedro II to abdicate. Brazil became a federal republic.

Chapter 10

Coming of Age

THE STORY of modern Brazil begins in 1930, when Getulio Vargas,* who had been governor of the state of Rio Grande do Sul, set up a revolutionary regime. Vargas ruled with a strong hand. This made people fear Vargas as a dictator. But he also took steps to make life better for the working man.

For years one of Brazil's biggest problems was coffee. Some years Brazil produced more coffee than the entire world could possibly drink. With so much coffee flooding world markets, its price dropped sharply. To try to get people to drink more, coffee growers almost had to give it away, and the whole Brazilian economy suffered.

To prevent these violent economic depressions, the Vargas government agreed to buy much of the country's coffee crop. Of course the government had no use for so much coffee. It didn't even have a place to store it. It solved that problem by burning it or dumping it in the ocean.

When it comes to knowing how to dry coffee beans in the sun, Brazilians are experts. And well they should be, for their country produces more coffee than any other.

In the six years after 1931, Vargas' government bought and destroyed almost a third of the coffee harvest. Such a step didn't solve the long-range problem. But it kept coffee workers busy raising beans which would be burned rather than brewed, and it kept world prices high for the coffee which didn't get burned or dumped.

Vargas put in a new constitution. Manufacturing was encouraged. Government money was funneled into building new factories. Though democracy didn't flourish under Vargas, Brazil's economy did.

The world of the arts began hearing about such musicians as Heitor Villa-Lobos.* It began appreciating Brazil's painters, architects, and novelists.

Vargas ruled as he pleased for a period of about 20 years. He was thrown out of office by a military coup in 1945, but five years later he was back in power when the military permitted new elections to be held. In 1954 his regime again was threatened with a military take-over. Vargas, faced with the loss of power, committed suicide.

Though he was a dictator, Vargas won the affection of Brazil's people. Today he stands as a symbol of Brazilian nationalism. Statues of him are found throughout Brazil.

Following Vargas was a series of left-leaning presidents. In the next 10 years, the *cruzeiro** — the Brazilian "dollar" — swiftly fell in value. Brazil's national debt rose rapidly. Then inflation forced people like Marcia's parents to spend more and more money to buy their families such basic essentials as food and clothing. In 1964 the army again stepped into Brazilian politics. It staged a revolution and ousted the democratically elected government. However, it was a distinctly Brazilian-type revolution. No one was killed or wounded.

Chapter 11

Soldiers and Slums

MANY OFFICERS of Latin America's armed forces regard themselves as guardians of their country. They're among the few in their nation who are educated, and most people respect them. Many professional military men are deeply patriotic, and at times the armed forces have prevented a country from falling into chaos.

Often, however, the officers are allied with the country's landowners and other wealthy people. Often, too, the career military officer in Latin America confuses public patriotism with respect for his uniform. The ups and downs of Brazil's military is a good example of how military men often misjudge their authority.

A few years back, some Brazilian army officers decided that Brazilians, especially students, were not showing enough respect to the military. Some

For many Brazilians, the road out of poverty is a long, uphill climb. Above, dusty village in northeast of Brazil.

younger officers were especially irritated that girls sometimes were rude to them.

One group in dress uniforms approached a number of girls sunning themselves on Rio de Janeiro's Copacabana Beach. The officers politely asked the girls for dates. The girls responded by calling the young officers a bunch of "gorillas."

No matter how hard it was to swallow, the military men could take such abuse from pretty girls. But when a member of Brazil's lawmaking body, the Chamber of Deputies, added his voice in criticism, it was too much. He made a speech in which he advised Brazilian mothers not to let their daughters go out with military men.

Such a strong public attack on the military isn't advisable in most of Latin America. "A Latin American politician who deliberately insults the military men in his country is out of his mind," observed one Brazilian army officer.

The lawmaker soon paid the price for taking on the nation's entire armed forces. As a legislator he had congressional immunity — the right of lawmakers to say things in Congress which they couldn't legally say outside. The military government first asked Congress to waive — or suspend — his immunity. But Congress refused to go along with this. The government took the next step. It dissolved Congress — all because of a lawmaker's views on girls dating army officers.

Like the people of Brazil, many other Latin Americans have spent long years under military dictators. Some said that this because Latin Americans had little taste for democracy.

"We Latins have always had a special feeling about the military," says one wealthy Brazilian. "There's something in our blood that makes us love parades and uniforms."

Yet in Brazil, as elsewhere, that special feeling faded. The new military leaders showed they were no better—and often worse—at solving problems than the civilians they overthrew. In the 1970's, the military leaders started ambitious but unwise development programs in hopes of spurring prosperity. But prices and unemployment soared, and the economy went into a tailspin. The only way the government could pay its bills was by borrowing money—about $100 billion—from foreign banks.

Brazil seemed nearly paralyzed by its leaders' lack of common sense. As its support faded, the regime promoted peaceful elections. Finally, in 1985, Dr. Tancredo de Almeida Neves was elected president. He was Brazil's first civilian president in 21 years. Brazilians showed their joy by dancing in the streets.

Within days, Brazilians faced a dramatic political crisis. Surgery forced the immensely popular Neves, 75, to miss his inauguration. Brazilians waited anxiously as Neves battled his illnesses. When he died following yet another emergency operation, some feared political upheaval would occur.

But Brazilians are a practical people who value stability. They stayed calm as Vice President José Sarney took power. The military had no excuse to intervene.

That peaceful reaction was typical of Brazilians. Even the nation's revolutions have usually been as bloodless as its bullfights. In Brazilian bullfights, the bull is never killed.

Double-check

Review

1. What is Brazil named after?

2. Who was brought to Brazil to work its sugar and cotton fields?

3. What was the greatest accomplishment of Dom Pedro II's rule?

4. How did the Brazilian government solve the problem of not having a place to store the coffee it bought?

5. Why are Brazilian revolutions said to be like Brazilian bullfights?

Discussion

1. Chapter 9 calls Brazil a "bubbling pot" because of its mixing of different races. The U.S. has often been called a "melting pot" for the millions of immigrants who settled here. How do the U.S. and Brazil seem similar in this regard? How are they different? Will either change? Why, or why not?

2. Chapter 10 points out, "Though he was a dictator, Vargas won the affection of Brazil's people." Why do you think Vargas was able to do this? What might be some advantages of government by dictatorship? What might be some disadvantages?

3. How do you think most people in the U.S. feel about soldiers and the military establishment? How is this similar to, or different from, the way Brazilians feel about the military? What factors in each country's history might help to explain their reactions to military parades and uniforms?

Activities

1. Some students might research and report to the rest of the class on how Brazilian coffee is grown, harvested, and processed for shipment to the U.S. and other countries.

2. In 1980 Brazil became the world leader among all countries trying to reduce their dependence on imported petroleum — primarily because the Iran-Iraq war cut off its major source of petroleum. Some students might research and report to the rest of the class on the Brazilian development of cars and other vehicles that run on alcohol instead of gasoline.

3. Two small groups of students might hold an informal debate in front of the rest of the class on whether or not the military should play a large, or small, role in the political life of a country.

Skills

	A. Slavery is abolished in Brazil.
1497–1498	B. Dom Pedro II abdicates.
1500	C. Cabral sights Brazil.
Late 1600's	
1807–1821	D. Vargas begins his rule.
1822	E. Da Gama finds a water route to the Indies.
1831–1889	F. Dom João governs from Brazil.
1888	G. Brazilian gold is discovered.
1889	H. Brazil proclaims its independence from Spain.
1930	
1954	I. The *cruzeiro* falls sharply in value.
1954–1964	J. Dom Pedro is crowned emperor.
1985	K. Vargas commits suicide.
	L. Dom Pedro II rules Brazil.
	M. Brazil returns to democratic rule.

Chapters 9 through 11 describe each of the events listed above. Using the timeline above, go back through the chapters to do the following on a separate sheet of paper.

1. Write the years given above down the left side of your paper.

2. Using the dates and events described in the chapter, write the letter of each event next to the year in which it happened. Some dates might include more than one of the events listed above. (Events are *not* in the correct order in the list above.)

THE LAND

Varied and forever changing, Latin America defies summing up in a few words. Bounded by immense oceans, cut by wide rivers, and topped by tall mountains, it seems a land of endless vistas. River steamer at mouth of mighty Amazon River (left). Old train chugs its way through Andes Mountains (below).

*NATURE: With its lofty peaks, steaming jungles,
roaring waterfalls, and glistening glaciers,
Latin America contains a wealth of natural wonders.*

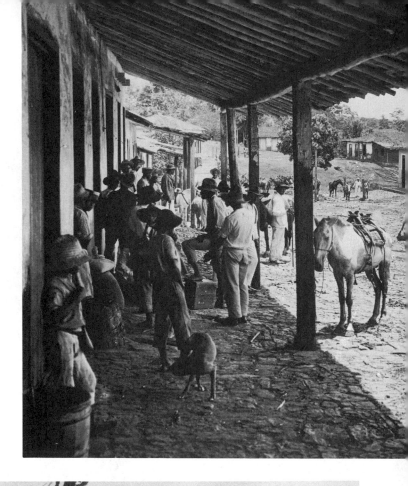

LAND USE: Man and his animals use land:
Brazilian farm village (top left), shore of Chilean
lake (bottom left), Peruvian llama caravan (above),
and Argentinian horse and cattle ranch (below).

URBAN: Cities grace or mar landscape — or do both.
Brasilia's Congress building (top left), Mexico
City's University (above), and Rio de Janeiro's beach
(below) are impressive. Not so are the slums
(below left) which scar many Latin American cities.

THE PEOPLE

Original inhabitants of Latin America were Indian. Here are Mexican (above) and Peruvian (right) Indians. European settlers were Spanish and Portuguese at first, later others. Numbers of black slaves were brought to Brazil as early as 1535.

FAITH: *Bride follows groom (left) after Peruvian
wedding. Mexican (above) makes floral arch
for church. Venezuelan boy (below) at church.*

HOME: In the villages, life is not easy. But things are done in tried and tested ways — tested, sometimes, over hundreds of years. Mexican women (above) wash clothes in stream. An Indian woman of Peru prepares a meal. But for children like these in village in Panama, there are friends and games to occupy the days.

POVERTY: Most Latin Americans are poor. Ecuadorian father and children (above) sleep on sidewalk. Widowed Ecuadorian mother (above right) must provide for family. Many Panamanians (right) live in ghetto and wait for jobs that aren't there.

THE ECONOMY

Latin America is still largely agricultural, although mines provide much income and industry is developing. Coffee (below) is the staple of many Latin economies. In towns and villages, people buy foodstuffs and other goods in open-air markets.

WORK: Bolivian boatbuilders (above) make reed craft. Venezuelan boatman (below) ends day. Ecuadorian shepherd (upper right) tends sheep, llamas. Peruvian women (right) thresh, winnow barley.

DISTRIBUTION: Cuban sugar cane worker
(above) hauls cane to mill. Bolivian women (below)
buy fruits and vegetables at outdoor market. Chilean
grape pickers (right) carry wine grapes to press.

VARIED TASKS: Chilean
longshoreman (left) loads copper
bars into ship's hold. Brazilian
steel mill (above) uses native
ores. Venezuelan workers (below)
unload rock from barge.
Brazilian machinist (right)
tools auto engine blocks.

THE
CULTURE

Latin America's distinctive culture is partly rooted in the past of its Indians. Machu Picchu (left) was built by Incas in Peru in 1500's. At Chichén Itzá,* Mexico, stands tall pyramid (below) erected by Mayans in pre-Christian times.

PAST: Toltecs in Mexico put up huge carved monoliths (left), which once supported temple. Inca weaver in Peru made poncho (below), using complex designs and symbols.

RELIGION: Musician
(below) entertains at Mexican religious fete. Ornate
church in Cuzco, Peru
(right), was built by
Spanish in 1600's.

RELIGION: Masked Venezuelan Indians (below left) take part in religious rite. Venezuelan Catholic woman (below) prays on bended knees.

CARNIVAL: In Bolivia (above) and Peru (upper right), it is mainly Indian festival. In Rio de Janeiro (lower right) and other Brazilian cities, there is much of Africa in festivities.

3
THE "EUROPEAN" COUNTRIES

Argentina:

"Live Ones" and "Hicks"

THE SECOND BIGGEST COUNTRY in South America, Argentina is a nation of immigrants. Most Argentines are descended from Spanish, Italian, German, English, Irish, or central European ancestors—or a mixture of these. In many ways, it seems quite European—especially its cities.

Unlike most of the people of Latin America, who are mainly of Indian or African stock mixed with European stock, Argentinians have little Indian or African heritage. This difference has shaped Argentina's history and culture.

Darío* is a teenager who lives in Buenos Aires,* the capital. Both his father's and mother's families came from Italy. His father is a photographer for the newspaper, *La Prensa.**

Since he lives in a big city, Darío's life is not too different from that of any other Argentine boy his age. For Argentina, like its neighbor, Brazil, is an urban nation — the majority of its people live in cities. About one third of all Argentina's population lives in Buenos Aires or its suburbs.

Other boys in Argentina would consider Darío lucky to live in Buenos Aires. One who lives in that city is known as a *porteño** — a resident of *"the* port." Nobody in Argentina asks which port. Everyone knows.

A man who lives in Buenos Aires is likely to think of himself as a *vivo* — a "live one." He knows what life's all about. Any Argentinian who lives outside Buenos Aires is regarded as a *campesino** — a country cousin, or a "hick." This goes even for people who live in other big Argentine cities.

As a result of their backgrounds, Argentinians tend to feel that they are people of the world rather than of one small part of it. The school Darío attends, for instance, is named for a president. But instead of a president of Argentina, it's named for Benito Juárez, once president of Mexico. Each year Darío's school has an assembly program to honor this Mexican revolutionary leader whom Argentinians have adopted as one of their own.

The arts of other nations thrive in Buenos Aires side by side with Argentinian culture. The Colón* Theatre in Buenos Aires is the biggest opera house in the world. It's also one of the fanciest. Its stage is so huge that 600 performers can crowd onto it at one time. The Colón also features ballet. Its opening nights are as splendid as those of the Paris Opera or the Metropolitan Opera in New York City. The city also has hundreds of art galleries.

A porteẍno who wants to see a play can go to any one of dozens of theaters in Buenos Aires. Many others feature the latest top films imported from Europe and the U.S. And among the country's own artists, Argenti-

Most Argentines are descended from European ancestors, and Argentine education stresses the nation's connection with world culture.

na's recent return to democracy has nurtured a tremendous flowering of artistic expression in film, books, drama, music, and the visual arts. In Buenos Aires, almost everyone considers himself or herself an artist, an art critic—or at the very least, an art lover.

Darío likes to go to movies and watch television. Most movies and TV programs he sees are made in the United States. Darío studies English at school, but so far he can speak only a few words. This doesn't interfere with his following the televised adventures.

113

❧ In Argentina, there are twice as many cattle as people.

The TV sound track has been dubbed so that the actors "speak" Spanish.

While neighboring Brazil has been a racial melting pot, Argentina, with its many foreign influences, has become more of a cultural mixing bowl. People from places such as Yugoslavia and Italy live side by side in Argentina's big cities. Each ethnic group follows certain customs brought over from "the old country." Yet many things about their daily lives—food, holidays, and other new traditions—mark them as Argentines, and not just transplanted foreigners.

A family that traces its roots to Italy, for example, undoubtedly will include spaghetti in its menu. But it's also likely to eat *asado,** an Argentine dish which consists of grilled beef heart, kidneys, and liver. And whatever their origin, Argentine children welcome the day of *Los Tres Reyes,** the Three Kings. They join the children of many Latin American countries in celebrating this holiday, which falls on January 6, the way kids in countries such as the United States celebrate Christmas.

In Latin America the Three Kings are assigned to the job of playing Santa Claus. Before going to sleep the night before, the children leave their shoes and socks in front of their bedroom doors. In the morning, they find them filled with presents — gifts from the Three Kings, of course.

Darío, lucky to be living in Buenos Aires, is twice lucky. His uncle owns a ranch in the country.

Darío visits this ranch during his summer vacation — in the months of December, January, and February. Summer begins just before Christmas in coun-

114

The gaucho, the Argentine cowboy, played a big part in developing Argentina — and still does. This one tends a herd on the Pampa.

tries like Argentina, which lie south of the Equator. The school year there begins in March, a time when U.S. students begin to look forward to the end of school.

On the ranch, Darío trades his city clothes for the outfit of a *gaucho*,* or cowboy. He wears baggy trousers and soft leather boots. The gauchos try to teach Darío to use the lasso, but so far he's better at talking about it than using it.

The gaucho life is still close to the hearts of many

115

Argentinians. The gaucho not only played a big part in the country's history. He still plays a big part in its economy. In Argentina, there are twice as many cattle as people, and beef is one of the country's chief exports.

Today's gaucho, however, leads a much more peaceful life than those of years past. For the frontier days of Argentina were perhaps even more violent than those of America's Wild West.

The Spaniards, who began arriving in Argentina shortly after 1500, soon discovered that the Indians living there were among the most stubborn fighters in the New World. Long before the Spaniards clashed with the Indians of Argentina, the Incas to the north had tried to subdue them — and had given up.

The Spaniards didn't find it any easier to impose their will on the Indians than the Incas had. Though the colonists killed them by the thousands, the war-like Indians kept coming back for more. They probably would have been stamped out altogether if it had not been for some kindhearted missionaries.

These religious men were members of the Franciscan and Jesuit orders of the Roman Catholic Church. They had a radical idea of how to try to solve the problem. Instead of using force against the Indians, they asked, why not try leaving them alone?

The missionaries finally persuaded the authorities to establish reservations, in which the Indians governed themselves. White men were barred from the reservations.

This idea worked where guns and swords had failed. Thus began an early example of "peaceful coexistence." But for the Indians, it was almost too late. Today there are only about 15,000 full-blooded Indians left in Argentina, chiefly in Patagonia, the southern, and less habitable, end of the country.

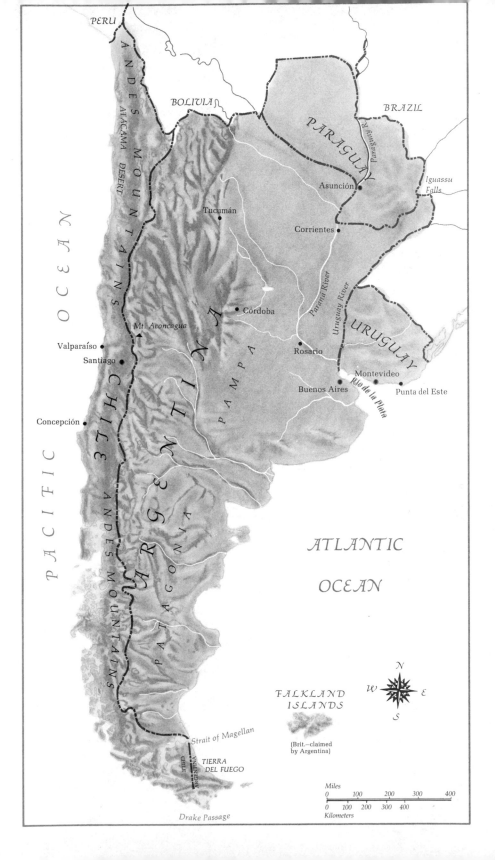

PERU

BOLIVIA

BRAZIL

PARAGUAY

ANDES MOUNTAINS

ATACAMA DESERT

Asunción

Tucumán

Corrientes

Iguassu
Falls

Paraguay River

Paraná River

Uruguay River

URUGUAY

PACIFIC

OCEAN

Mt. Aconcagua

Córdoba

PAMPA

Valparaíso

Santiago

Rosario

Montevideo

Río de la Plata

Punta del Este

CHILE

ARGENTINA

Concepción

Buenos Aires

ANDES MOUNTAINS

PATAGONIA

ATLANTIC

OCEAN

N
W · E
S

Strait of Magellan

CHILE

ARGENTINA

TIERRA
DEL FUEGO

FALKLAND
ISLANDS

(Brit.—claimed
by Argentina)

Drake Passage

Miles
0   100   200   300   400

0   100 200 300 400
Kilometers

José de San Martín, on white horse, leads the revolutionary forces across the Andes Mountains to attack the Spaniards.

JOSÉ DE SAN MARTÍN

THE STORY OF José de San Martín* is as familiar to Argentine boys and girls as the story of George Washington is to young people in the U.S.

San Martín was one of the great soldiers who helped South America gain its independence from Spain. He was born in a small village in northern Argentina in 1778. When he was seven, his aristocratic Spanish parents returned to their homeland, taking José with them.

San Martín spent 22 years in the Spanish army, rising to the rank of lieutenant colonel. But all this time he remained loyal to Argentina, the country of his birth.

In 1812 he heard that an independence movement was stirring in Buenos Aires. He returned to Argentina and offered his services to the revolutionary forces.

Argentina declared its independence in 1816. Much of Spain's power in South America was concentrated in Peru. "The war," San Martín said, "will not end until we are in Lima* [Peru's capital]."

To reach Lima, San Martín decided he had first to drive the Spaniards from neighboring Chile. Once he had set up a friendly government there, he could use Chile as a springboard to invade Peru by sea.

San Martín was a brilliant military planner. For three

years he organized and drilled his army. Then in 1817 he led 5,200 men across the Andes to help Chilean patriots led by Bernardo O'Higgins.

San Martín's forces caught the Spaniards off guard. His soldiers twice defeated the enemy in battle. San Martín entered Santiago,* Chile, in triumph on February 15, 1817. The next step was to invade Peru.

Again San Martín began long preparations. He spent almost two years assembling a fleet to carry out this task. He set sail for Lima in August 1820, and, on July 9, 1821, he entered the former Spanish bastion and proclaimed independence for all Peru.

The people of Lima offered San Martín the title of "Protector." But San Martín was a soldier and had no desire for political power. He favored setting up a monarchy under a constitution. First of all, though, he believed his job of defeating the Spanish throughout the southern part of South America should be completed.

The Spanish forces in Lima had retreated into the highlands of Peru. San Martín decided he needed the help of another great South American liberator, Simón Bolívar,* to pursue them.

At the time, Bolívar's army was marching south to liberate Ecuador. The two great leaders of South American independence held a famous meeting in Ecuador in July 1822.

Just what happened at that meeting remains a mystery. One thing was apparent: the two men reached no agreement on South America's future. And this failure had a profound effect on San Martín.

For 10 years he had fought for South America's independence. All the while his political enemies accused him of seeking personal power. At last he became tired and discouraged. Declaring that Bolívar was "not the man we imagined him to be," San Martín returned to Lima and, in September 1822, handed in his resignation to the Peruvian congress. Going into exile, he wrote:

"I am tired of being called a tyrant . . . of having the people say that I want to be king, emperor, or even the devil."

Chapter 13

Argentina the Proud

EVEN WHEN THEY were deprived of democracy, the Argentinians have been a proud people. Pride is a trademark found throughout much of Latin America. But Argentine pride has a seriousness all its own.

This culturally diverse country has many things of which to be proud. Argentinians have proved that people of many different backgrounds and religions can live together in peace. About 95 percent of the people can read and write—the highest literacy rate in Latin America. Argentina's people enjoy the highest standard of living in the entire region. And their beautiful country has some of the most spectacular scenery to be found anywhere.

In the Andes Mountains, which run along the Chilean border, are the six highest peaks in the Americas. The highest of these is snow-capped Mt. Aconcagua,* 22,834 feet tall. Iguassú* Falls are so tremendous that

Sweeping the sky of western Argentina are the icy peaks of the Andes Mountains, the world's second highest range. These majestic peaks form a vast stone barricade to easy travel between Argentina and its next-door neighbor, Chile.

they make Niagara Falls seem like a trickle. The waters of Niagara drop a mere 167 feet and are only 3,500 feet wide. The water that goes hurtling down over Iguassú — which means "the Great Water" in the Guaraní* Indian language — falls 200 feet and measures 8,100 feet, more than a mile and a half in width.

As beautiful as these natural wonders are, many Argentinians think the most imposing sight of all is the Pampa. *Pampa,** in Spanish, means "plains." Here fields of wheat or lush green grass stretch as far as the eye can see. Its moderate weather, plentiful rain, and fertile soil make the Pampa one of the richest cattle-raising and farming regions of the world. This plain rises gradually from the Atlantic coast and sprawls

121

◆§ Argentinians say that the Pampa is "so kind that just tickling her with a hoe will cause her to laugh with a harvest."

for thousands of square miles across central Argentina. It is on the Pampa that Darío's uncle has his ranch.

Argentinians say that the Pampa is a land "so kind that just tickling her with a hoe will cause her to laugh with a harvest." On the Pampa are about nine tenths of Argentina's farmland, three fourths of its industry, and the city of Buenos Aires. Living upon it are more than two thirds of Argentina's people.

Cattle and crops raised on the Pampa make Argentina one of the biggest wheat-growing and meat-exporting countries in the world. There are many other crops grown in this country, which is so long from north to south (2,294 miles) that almost every kind of climate can be found in its borders.

Argentina exports such items as wool, animal hides, cereals, wheat meal and flour, and animal by-products. The number of items made from these by-products is surprising. They include powdered fertilizers; casings for sausages; hoofs, horns, and bones for buttons, knife handles, and glue; cattle hair for upholstery; and ear hair for paint brushes.

Argentina's prosperity began in the 1930's, when it started large-scale exporting to the U.S. and Europe. By the end of World War II, the national treasury was bursting. People thought Argentina would soon become the strongest and wealthiest country in Latin America.

In 1946 a colonel named Juan Perón* took office. Perón became one of the most popular leaders in Latin American history. Though he died in 1974, his long

Out on the Pampa space is silent and solitude is sweet. Much of the land is owned by large landholders, who graze herds of cattle in the millions over the lush expanses.

shadow still hangs over Argentina's political life.

With his wife Eva, Perón built up enormous popularity among Argentina's workers. He boosted wages and saw to it that the poor received medical and other benefits. He poured money into other highly publicized projects to help out Argentina's poor. But Perón also brought Argentina to the edge of bankruptcy.

In 1955, Argentina's army revolted and threw Perón out of office. But even in exile, Perón was still the most important person in Argentina. One government after another fell because of Perón's followers. These *Peronistas** wanted one thing: Perón's return. Finally, an aging Perón returned to office in 1973. He died after 10 months, and his third wife, Isabel, succeeded him for nearly two years.

The military regime that booted her out and controlled the nation from 1976 to 1983 was brutal. A crackdown on all opponents led to arrests, tortures, and killings. Officials kept no records, but an estimated 6,000 to 30,000 citizens simply disappeared.

June of 1982 bought what may have been the last straw. In April, Argentina tried to seize the British-held Falkland Islands, 250 miles off its coast. By June, British troops defeated the Argentinians and forced them to surrender. The humiliated generals sped the return to civilian government.

In 1983, Argentinians celebrated the inauguration of President Raúl Alfonsín. Alfonsín began his career as a champion of human rights during the dangerous years of military rule. But restoring human rights isn't the only issue he has had to deal with.

The Falklands defeat still simmers in many Argentinians' minds. And the financial crisis Alfonsín inherited from the generals still threatens to boil over. Many fear that if he can't solve the country's economic problems, Alfonsín—and perhaps even Argentine democracy—may lose the people's support.

Double-check

Review

1. When does summer begin in countries like Argentina?

2. Where do most of the full-blooded Indians left in Argentina live?

3. Who was José de San Martín?

4. What makes the Pampa one of the richest cattle-raising and farming regions in the world?

5. After 1955 what one thing did the *Peronistas* want?

Discussion

1. How do you think the Indians in Argentina feel today about Spaniards and other European settlers? How is the story of the Indians in Argentina similar to the story of Indians in the U.S.? How is it different?

2. Do you think San Martín wanted to be a king or an emperor? Why, or why not? Why do you think San Martín remained loyal to Argentina during his 22 years in the Spanish army? What builds loyalty to a country?

3. In the late 1970's, many wealthy and upper-middle-class people in Argentina tried to ignore the unstable and often violent political situation in their country. Can people really do this? Why, or why not? Why do you think those people tried to ignore politics? Would you have agreed with their reasons?

Activities

1. A committee of students might prepare a bulletin board display and/or oral reports on various aspects of life in Argentina, including art, music, architecture, language, religion, dress, crafts, customs, politics, and the economy.

2. Some students might read the play *Evita* about Eva Perón; then the whole class might listen to the musical soundtrack from the play, while those who have read the play explain the significance of the songs.

3. Several students might take turns role-playing the historic meeting between Bolívar and San Martín in July 1822. Each skit could offer a different version of what happened, and then the class could vote on which interpretation they think explains the two leaders' failure to reach an agreement on South America's future.

Skills

March 1978– February 1979

Page 73

ARGENTINA—Continued

Politics and government

Argentina in agony. S Kinzer. New Repub 179:17-21 D 23 '78

Between repression and reform: a stranger's impressions of Argentina and Brazil. F. Stern. bibl f For Aff 56:800-18 Jl '78

Can Argentina really move forward this time? E. McCrary. Bus W p58+ My 22 '78

Demonology in Argentina. L. Zeldin. Progressive 42:8+ F '78

Legacy of Perón. P. Witonski. New Repub 178:13-17 Je 17 '78

Revolt and repression in Argentina. D. Rock. Cur Hist 74:57-60+ F '78

Religious institutions and affairs

See also
Catholic Church in Argentina
Church and state in Argentina

ARGENTINE fiction
Visit from Julio Cortázar; interview, ed by F. MacShane. J. Cortázar, por N Y Times Bk R 83:3+ F 12 '78

ARGENTINE scientists. See Scientists, Argentina

Abbreviations:

bibl f — bibliographical footnotes

Bus W — *Business Week*

Cur Hist — *Current History*

D — December

ed — edited

F — February

For Aff — *Foreign Affairs*

Jl — July

Je — June

My — May

New Repub — *New Republic*

NY Times Bk R —

    New York Times Book Review

por — portrait

+ — continued on later pages

Use the above material from Readers' Guide to Periodical Literature *and information in Chapters 12 and 13 to answer the following questions.*

1. In which of the following publications will you find the articles listed in *Readers' Guide?*

    (a) newspapers (b) magazines (c) books

2. How many articles are listed above?

    (a) three (b) six (c) seven

3. How long a period of time is covered by this edition of *Readers' Guide?*

    (a) two years (b) two months (c) one year

4. Under which letter of the alphabet would you look in *Readers' Guide* for listings of articles about Argentine scientists?

    (a) S (b) R (c) A

5. In which magazine would you find an article about a colonel who took office in Argentina in 1946, or his wife?

    (a) *New Republic* (b) *Foreign Affairs* (c) *Progressive*

126

Chapter 14

Uruguay:

Too Much Wool

ORA IS A 15-year-old girl who lives in the center of Uruguay's capital, Montevideo.* Sometimes her family goes to the big resort called Punta del Este,* not far from Montevideo.

At Punta del Este, Ora has a choice of two beaches. One, the "Gentle Beach," is sheltered from the wind so its waves are gentle. The other, the "Rough Beach," is directly on the wave-tossed Atlantic Ocean.

But Ora might not be doing quite so much swimming in the future. Uruguay has been hit by inflation, and her family has had to tighten its purse strings. Uruguay is suffering the same kind of economic pains that Brazil periodically goes through when it raises more coffee than the world can drink.

What causes Uruguay's inflation? Too much wool, for one thing.

Tiny Uruguay, wedged between Brazil and Argentina, has no oil. It has no coal, no iron, no heavy industries. It has sheep, cattle, and wheat. These and

127

such products as wool sheared from the sheep are about all the country has to sell to world markets.

Uruguay once was a country mainly populated by wild livestock. In 1603 the governor of neighboring Paraguay shipped about a hundred head of cattle and another hundred horses downstream and left them to graze on the uninhabited but fertile banks of the Uruguay River. Many of these animals ran wild.

These wild horses and cattle became so numerous that they attracted gauchos from Argentina. These cowboys roamed over the land, rounding up the wild animals and selling their hides for leather.

This trade in hides, in turn, attracted merchants from Buenos Aires. As this wild country became crowded with cattlemen, boundaries were fixed. This was the beginning of the huge ranches which still form the basis of Uruguay's economy.

Though most of Uruguay's money comes from ranches and farmlands, it's far from a backward country. This rather small South American nation is dominated by the city of Montevideo, which contains almost half of the entire country's inhabitants.

Uruguay has up-to-date schools. It has a very low illiteracy rate for a Latin American nation (about six per cent). The University of Montevideo has a famous medical school which attracts students from all South America.

About 3,000 miles of paved roads fan out from Montevideo. These are some of the best highways in South America. Railroads also link the capital to smaller cities. Cattle and sheep, wheat and wool are transported on these rails to the big city. From Montevideo much of this freight is shipped abroad on the ships which steam in and out of the city's big harbor.

For years, Uruguay's economy was supported by the world-wide demand for wool. But when chemists began discovering and developing "miracle fibers," the bottom dropped out of Uruguay's wool market — and its economy. The country has not yet recovered from this blow.

Despite Uruguay's inflation, Ora's life hasn't changed drastically. Dinner, the main meal of the day, is still served promptly at nine. There's always plenty of meat. Ora and her brothers are served dishes like beef or veal roasted on a skewer. Or they have several different kinds of meat such as liver, kidney, and sausages roasted over hot coals. Or there might be beef roasted with the hide still on the meat, a dish that takes a long time to prepare.

Whatever the meat is, it'll be washed down with lots of *maté,** the strong tea favored by the people of Uruguay as well as Argentina. Maté is sipped through a silver straw from a special cup.

"I go to a private school, the Crandon Institute," says Ora. "It's run by people from the United States. Both Uruguayan and U.S. boys and girls are in my classes. I study Spanish literature, world history, algebra, geometry, chemistry, physics, drawing, home economics, music, and gym. We have classes six days a week, but only in the morning on Saturday."

Though Ora's family has plenty to eat and can afford a good education for the children, they've tried to cut such extras as frequent trips to the beach. The cost of living in Uruguay jumped over 60 percent a year during the early 1980's. Things cost more than twice as much as they had two years before. With such high inflation rates, people find it hard to make ends meet or to plan the future. Still, middle-class families like Ora's live well, and the jumps in the cost of living were much larger in earlier years.

The people most hurt by the country's economic woes are the residents of hundreds of slum villages

Uruguayan gauchos, in baggy pants and sombreros, pass around a cup of maté, the strong tea favored by Uruguayans. Maté is sipped through a silver straw from a special cup.

throughout Uruguay. They live in makeshift housing. They find whatever work they can and eat whatever— and whenever—they can.

The slum villages are located in a country which long ago became known for its progressive laws. Uruguay was the first Latin American country to pass extensive labor legislation and to establish a social security system. But few of its people have thrived despite these ambitious welfare programs. Indeed, some economists blame many of Uruguay's problems on some of the very laws designed to produce a state in which there would be plenty for all.

Uruguay's problems are acute today. Much of the government's revenue goes to support the welfare programs. To regulate its many activities, the government keeps growing. A huge percentage of the country's entire working force is now employed by the government.

The government controls electricity and the refining of petroleum, which it must import. It manufactures cement. It operates a big meat-packing plant. It runs the railroads and controls the banking and insurance businesses.

So many government pay checks cause a huge financial drain on Uruguay's taxpayers. And so many hands in government often result in inefficiency. Added to this are frequent battles between the military government, which took control in 1973, and left-wing guerrillas trying to overthrow the government.

But recent signs indicate that Uruguay's long run of bad luck and clumsy government may be changing for the better. In 1985, Uruguayans elected their first civilian government since 1972. In their early steps to renew stability, they can draw on a long tradition of tolerance. A century ago, the English author W. H. Hudson marveled at the Uruguayan Pampa: "Here the lord of many leagues of land and herds of unnumbered sits down to talk with the hired shepherd . . . and no class or caste differences divide them, no consciousness of their widely different positions chills the warm current of sympathy between two human hearts."

Chapter 15

Chile:
The Rich Lieutenant

STRETCHING SOUTH OF Peru and Bolivia is Chile, a stringbean country 2,650 miles long and only 225 miles wide at its widest point. It was once considered Spain's least valued possession. While countries like Peru and Bolivia were producing silver and gold, all Chile seemed to produce was problems. Now this country is one of the most industrialized nations in South America.

Like Argentina, its neighbor across the mountains, Chile is not an "Indian" country. Like settlers in Argentina, the Europeans who first arrived in Chile found the land occupied by warlike Indians who gave it up only after a fierce struggle. Today few Indians exist in Chile.

The majority of Chileans are of Spanish descent. But, again like Argentina, this country has a great variety in its population. The ancestors of many Chileans came from nations like Britain, Germany, and Italy.

Hernán is a 14-year-old school boy in Chile's capital, Santiago. His great-grandfather came from Yugoslavia in the late 1800's, looking for gold. He didn't find any, but he remained in Chile and started a family.

Hernán comes from a family of teachers. His father is a professor at the University of Santiago and his mother teaches at the public school which Hernán attends with his two brothers.

"My family lives in the eastern part of Santiago, called Nunoa," says Hernán. "Our house is built of concrete, with flower gardens in front and in the rear. From our house we can see the Andes."

Hernán is studying Spanish, English, French, math, biology, history, geography, physics, chemistry, music, art, woodworking, and gym. If you think that's a heavy schedule, you're right. Chile has put more emphasis on education than many Latin American nations. As a result, it has an unusually high literacy rate for this region — about 90 per cent.

Like many other Chilean teenagers, Hernán at 14 has more freedom than teenagers two and three years older in other Latin American countries. For example, teenagers in Mexico or Argentina would not normally be allowed to date without a chaperone. In the cities of Chile, however, a girl of 13 or 14 may go with friends to the movies or double date. In the villages, however, young people are under stricter supervision. There, the traditional way of meeting is the *paseo*,* or stroll. On Sundays after church, young people walk back and forth along the main plaza of their town. If a boy is interested in a girl, he may speak to her after passing her three or four times on the *paseo*.

Nine out of 10 Chileans live in the temperate central area. This area, about the size of Kansas, is Chile's Central Valley — Chile's version of the Argentine Pampa. Here farmers grow wheat, potatoes, oats, corn, barley, rice, beans, and onions. Despite the valley's rich soil, however, it doesn't produce enough food for all Chile's people. The nation has had to buy huge amounts of food each year from other countries.

Partly at fault is the *hacienda** system — which has plagued most of Latin America throughout its history. A hacienda is a large farm owned by one family from generation to generation. Only a few years ago, almost 70 per cent of Chile's best farmlands were owned by only four per cent of the people.

The haciendas were worked by tenant farmers and their families. In return for his work, the farmer got a small part of the crop. He turned over most of the harvest to the hacienda owner.

In the 1960's, the Chilean government tried to reform the hacienda system. The government broke up some of the largest estates and distributed the land among the peasants. Some of these peasants came from families which had worked for hundreds of years on the same haciendas. Now, at last, they were farming their own land. But the program fell far short of its goals.

In 1970 Dr. Salvador Allende* was elected president of Chile. The election created much interest both in Latin American and the U.S. Allende was inspired by the theories of Karl Marx, a German philosopher in the 1800's. In fact, Allende was the first Marxist ever chosen in free elections to lead a major democratic nation. He was also highly critical of the U.S.

Under Allende, Chile's government tried a radical solution to its problems. It broke up more haciendas and took over many key industries. One result was an

134

These women often get steamed up over their jobs. They're shelling clams for canning, one phase of a food-processing industry which makes up about a fourth of Chile's industrial output.

inflation that ate deeply into the resources of Chileans. The economic troubles led to widespread violence between pro-Allende and anti-Allende Chileans.

For years, the people of Chile had taken pride that their army had stayed out of politics. But that tradition ended in 1973, when a group of officers took control of the country. Allende was killed in the revolt, and the military government rounded up and exe-

Beneath the dust-dry Atacama desert lie vast copper deposits. To get at them requires mines such as 1,000-foot-deep Chuquicamata (above), largest open-pit copper mine on earth. To give you some idea of the size of the mine, note the tiny railway cars at the floor of the mine.

cuted many of his top supporters. In the years after the military take-over, Chileans were subjected to strict rule and few democratic freedoms.

Today, the great mass of Chileans are clustered in the central section of the country. To the south is a bleak windswept plateau that stretches down practically to the Antarctic Circle. To the north is

136

the forbidding Atacama desert which reaches practically into the tropics. In this barren northland, there are parts in which rain has never been recorded. Yet here is where some of the greatest natural wealth in South America is located.

There is a story that in the early 19th century, a Spanish army lieutenant stationed in Chile found himself deeply in debt and decided to desert. Making his way toward the Andes and Argentina, he stumbled upon a mass of green-tinted rock. The lieutenant knew a little about minerals and realized that he had found the answer to his debts.

He returned to Chile with the news that he had discovered a tremendous deposit of copper. Because of his exciting news, he was welcomed back as a hero, not a deserter. Today Chile is one of the world's biggest copper mining countries, and one of its richest mines is *El Teniente,** "the lieutenant." It is one of the world's largest underground copper mines.

Mines such as this one have made Chile one of the world's leading exporters of copper. They have also turned the "stringbean" country into one of the leading industrial nations in Latin America. This industrial growth and the country's political troubles help explain why Chile has become a focus of attention in newspapers around the world.

Chileans are supposed to have the ability to laugh at themselves. But in recent years, they have had little to laugh at. Their nation suffers from crushing economic problems. Their government has one of the worst human-rights records in all of Latin America. General Augusto Pinochet* Ugarte, who took power in 1973, is an iron-fisted dictator. Widespread arrest and torture is common. Pinochet has sent hundreds of critics into "internal exile" at faraway detention camps. Few Chileans expect conditions to improve while he remains in charge.

Double-check

Review

1. What still forms the basis of Uruguay's economy?

2. When did the bottom drop out of Uruguay's wool market?

3. Who are the people most hurt by Uruguay's inflation?

4. What is a *hacienda*?

5. What helps to explain why Chile has become a focus of attention in newspapers around the world?

Discussion

1. What are some advantages of a country building its economy around one main product? What are some disadvantages? What kinds of products or services form the basis of your community's economy? What might happen to your community if demand for these goods or services fell off sharply?

2. Do you think W.H. Hudson's statement about human relationships on the Uruguayan Pampa might still be true? What aspects of Uruguayan culture might help to make it true? Which aspects might help to destroy such idealized relationships? Explain your answers.

3. How do the traditional ways of meeting and dating in Chile compare with those of your community? Which patterns do you think lead to better relationships? Why?

Activities

1. Two committees of students might prepare bulletin board displays and/or oral reports on aspects of life in Uruguay and Chile, including art, music, architecture, language, religion, dress, crafts, customs, politics, and the economies.

2. Some students might pretend to be Ora or one of her brothers. These students could write letters to imaginary friends in the U.S. telling how their family's life has been affected by Uruguay's inflation. Other students could then pretend to be the imaginary U.S. friends and write responses to the letters, telling how inflation in the U.S. has affected their lives.

3. Groups of students might take turns role-playing *paseo* scenes — first as they might occur in a Chilean village (as described in Chapter 15) and then as they might occur in your community.

Skills

USING AN INDEX

Cartagena, 165, 166, 171
Castro, Fidel, 198, 199–201
charros, 26–27
Chibcha Indians, 164–165,
    167
Chile, 118, 132–137, 142, 168
    copper, 136*–137
    culture, 133
    economy, 133–134
    population makeup, 132
Colombia, 142, 164–169,
    171
Columbus, Christopher, 176,
    183, 198
Copacabana, 61, 74

---

*Photograph.

Use the excerpt above from the Index and information in Chapters 14 and 15 to answer the following questions.

1. In what order are topics listed in an index?
(a) in order of importance   (b) by page numbers   (c) alphabetically

2. On what page might you find a photograph of a Chilean copper mine?
(a) page 118   (b) page 136   (c) page 137

3. On how many pages in this text is Chile's population makeup discussed?
(a) one   (b) two   (c) 132

4. On what page would you find the first mention of Chile?
(a) page 118   (b) page 136   (c) page 165

5. On what page or pages might you read about what a deserting Spanish army lieutenant discovered in the early 19th century?
(a) page 118   (b) pages 136–137   (c) page 174

4
THE "INDIAN" COUNTRIES

Chapter 16

People of the Sun

WHILE THE AZTEC civilization was thriving in what is now Mexico, another Indian empire was prospering far to the south, in the highlands of South America's Andes Mountains. This was the land of the Incas.

The Inca civilization in some ways was even more remarkable than that of the Aztecs. The Incas were scientific farmers. They learned to produce bigger crops with fertilizers. They built huge irrigation projects which brought water to arid fields from a hundred miles away. They turned the sides of mountains into terraced farmlands which stepped up almost to the snow line of the Andes' whitecapped peaks.

Under the Incas, all land was public and was doled out to families each year on the basis of their size. The government also required each farmer to store some of his crops in public storehouses. During lean

141

years, when crops were bad, this stored food was distributed to the needy.

Like the Aztecs, the Incas were great builders. They erected huge buildings of massive stones. Some stones weighed up to 200 tons. Yet they were fitted together without mortar so precisely that even today a visitor can't slip a knife blade between some of the big stones. This mortarless construction has survived this area's frequent earthquakes. Some modern buildings haven't.

The Inca network of highways ran from the capital city of Cuzco* to all parts of the empire. Some are still in use. In the mountains the Incas built suspension bridges to pass the road over canyons or rivers.

The Inca religion was, like the Aztec, a form of sun worship. The Incas believed that their emperor, or "Lord Inca," was a divine descendant of the sun. They offered him blood sacrifices, the way the Aztecs sought to please their own fierce sun god.

But the Incas weren't nearly as bloodthirsty as the Aztecs. Though an unlucky human being was sometimes chosen to die for the Lord Inca, most often a llama* would be sacrificed. These animals, which look something like a camel, are still used in the Andes as beasts of burden and to provide wool.

At the height of their power, the Incas ruled what is now Peru, Bolivia, Ecuador, Colombia, and parts of Chile and Argentina. This 380,000-square-mile area is about equal in size to France, Belgium, the Netherlands, Switzerland, Luxembourg, and Italy combined. More than five million Indians were under the authority of the Lord Inca in Cuzco.

Eleven years after Cortés invaded the capital of the Aztecs to the north, the Spanish conquistador Francisco Pizarro* set out to explore the land of the Incas. He had even fewer men than Cortés — only

◄§ Atahualpa could hardly believe his ears. A handful of white strangers had appeared from nowhere and demanded that he give up his birthright.

---

180 to Cortés' 500. But Pizarro, like Cortés, had great advantages over his opponents — firearms, horses, and an unquenchable will to conquer.

Pizarro landed on the north coast of Peru and crossed the mountains to search for Atahualpa,* the Lord Inca. Atahualpa was at his favorite resort town. With him was an army of about 30,000 men.

When Atahualpa heard of the tiny group marching toward him, he was curious, not alarmed. After all, what harm could Pizarro's men do to his thousands? To meet Pizarro he took only a few thousand warriors. He did not know that the Spaniards were preparing a deadly reception for him.

The Inca delegation which met the Spaniards that day carried only short clubs and slings. Pizarro, meanwhile, had arranged his soldiers in strategic positions around the village square. Shortly after Atahualpa met the Spaniards, a priest with Pizarro engaged the Lord Inca in a one-sided debate.

The priest immediately began telling the Lord Inca and his warriors about the Christian religion. He not only asked Atahualpa to accept the Christian faith; he also advised the Indian leader to recognize the Spanish king as his master.

Atahualpa could hardly believe his ears. A handful of white strangers had appeared from nowhere and suddenly demanded that he give up his birthright. After the priest had finished, Atahualpa pointed out to the intruders that this Spanish king might be a

Ancient walls near city of Cuzco display Inca building skills. Without benefit of mortar, Incas piled massive blocks atop one another, making the fit so tight that even today a knife can't be slipped between stones.

ruler in a distant country. But he, Atahualpa, ruled the very land upon which they stood. And, as for this new religion . . . the Lord Inca grabbed the Bible from the priest's hand and flung it to the ground.

Pizarro was prepared for just such a reaction. His men attacked the surprised Indians and cut them down by the hundreds. Pizarro himself captured Atahualpa.

Pizarro knew of the Incas' wealth and demanded ransom for the return of their chief. The Indians gathered as ransom a whole roomful of gold and silver. After collecting this bounty, Pizarro went back on his bargain and still held Atahualpa captive. The Inca leader was put on "trial." One charge against Atahualpa was that he had plotted to overthrow the

Spaniards. A second charge was that he had killed his own brother and had worshipped idols.

Atahualpa was found guilty and sentenced to death by being burned at the stake. At the last moment, he said he would become a Christian, and he was baptized. This saved him from being burned at the stake, but it did not save his life. On orders of Pizarro, Atahualpa was strangled to death. With him died the Inca empire.

☆ ☆ ☆ ☆ ☆ ☆ ☆ ☆ ☆

Today, four-and-a-half centuries after the fall of the Inca empire, Cuzco remains an Indian city. In Cuzco you see Indian history stamped on the faces of most of the people. Many of Cuzco's inhabitants are pure-blooded Indians. Others are mestizos.

Down the stone-paved lanes built by their Inca ancestors Indian women trudge wearing layers of long skirts and carrying big bundles in their shawls. On feast days the sandal-clad Indians don rainbow-colored ponchos and bowl-like hats.

The Peruvian people are proud of their Indian past. Walls built by the Incas still stand in and around Cuzco, and modern builders are forbidden by law to tear them down. Any new buildings which arise on these sites must be built around the old constructions.

Peruvians visit Cuzco to study the past, much as Americans visit such historical places as Boston, Philadelphia, or Williamsburg. At Cuzco some of them board a small train which chugs its way through the mountains to a city which, until recent years, had been lost for centuries.

Experts have called this city of *Machu Picchu** the most important archaeological discovery in South America. There's no doubt that it is one of the most popular tourist attractions on the continent. Some believe that when Pizzaro's men sacked the Inca capital of Cuzco, many Indians fled to this hideaway high in the mountains.

The people of Machu Picchu eventually disappeared or died out. The weight of centuries collapsed the village's thatched roofs. Vines climbed over its stone walls. Trees took root and further hid all traces of the quiet village.

In 1911 a young Yale professor decided to investigate stories of a "lost city" of the Incas. The professor, Hiram Bingham, led an expedition from Cuzco into the mountains. At the top of one mountain, they stumbled upon strange stones covered by brush.

"It was hard to see them," Bingham wrote, "for they were partly covered with trees and moss, the growth of centuries. But in the dense shadow, hiding in bamboo thickets and tangled vines, appeared here and there walls of white granite ashlars [square stones] carefully cut and exquisitely fitted together."

Archaeologists chopped away the tangled growth and hauled out the dirt which had sifted over Machu Picchu for generations. At last they uncovered the remains of its terraces, temples, and houses.

Parts of Machu Picchu stand today much as they did when they were first built. The thatched roofs are missing, but the stone walls are still strong. Walking down its streets, a visitor almost expects to see an ancient Inca priest, splendid in his fine robes, walking from one of the doorways to greet — or to challenge — him (see photo essay, page 102).

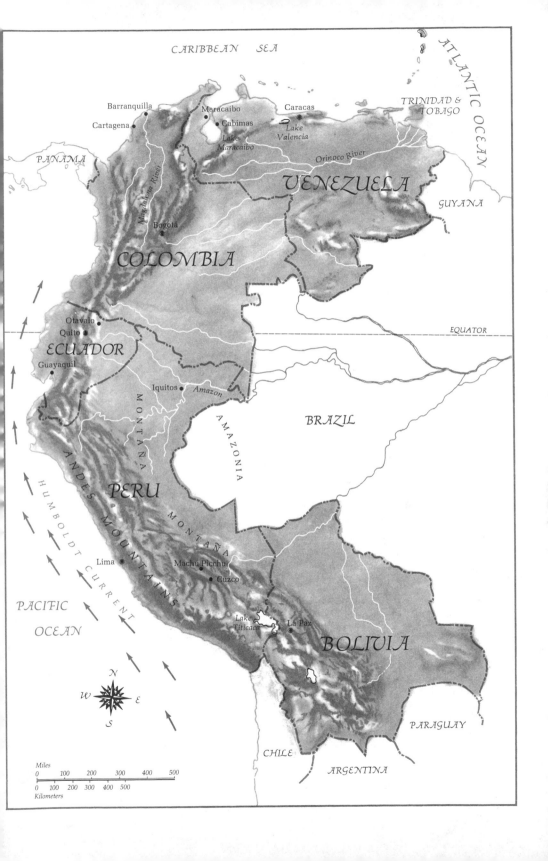

CARIBBEAN SEA

ATLANTIC OCEAN

Barranquilla
Cartagena
Maracaibo
Cabimas
Caracas
Lake Valencia

TRINIDAD & TOBAGO

PANAMA

Lake Maracaibo

Orinoco River

VENEZUELA

GUYANA

Magdalena River

Bogotá

COLOMBIA

Otavalo
Quito

EQUATOR

ECUADOR

Guayaquil

Iquitos
Amazon

BRAZIL

MONTAÑA

AMAZONIA

PERU

ANDES MOUNTAINS

MONTAÑA

HUMBOLDT CURRENT

Lima
Machu Picchu
Cuzco

PACIFIC OCEAN

Lake Titicaca
La Paz

BOLIVIA

N
W   E
S

PARAGUAY

CHILE

ARGENTINA

Miles
0   100   200   300   400   500
0   100   200   300   400   500
Kilometers

Chapter 17

Boom and Bust in Peru

CARLOS IS A 15-year-old boy who lives in Lima, capital and largest city of Peru. Like Mexico City, Lima is a mixture of old and new. Carlos' older brother attends the University of San Marcos. This university, founded in 1551, is, along with the University of Mexico, the oldest in the Americas. (The oldest university in the United States, Harvard, wasn't set up until 85 years later.)

Carlos' father is a doctor. His family, one of the oldest in Lima, lives in a fine old Spanish-style house. Like many such houses, it is built around a *patio*.

Yet many of Lima's houses are new, for this is another Latin American city that is growing fast. Each year thousands of people move to Lima, and the city's population now tops three million.

Carlos likes pop music, and his favorite sports are soccer and basketball. He lives within walking distance of school, and the first thing he does when he

Like most of South America's Indian republics, Peru is governed by a small group of wealthy whites. Above, the mayor of Lima (in top hat) and other influential Peruvians, at a celebration of Peru's Independence Day.

arrives home for lunch is to listen to a cassette by Michael Jackson on his tape player. Carlos keeps up with the latest music from around the world.

Lima boys usually play such games as basketball outdoors. Their games are seldom rained out. The Peruvian coast sometimes goes for years without rainfall. This area has a cloudy season, from June to October. But seldom do the clouds produce much rain.

The city of Lima lies less than a thousand miles south of the Equator, and its elevation is only about 500 feet. Yet its annual average temperature is only 67 degrees. The reason for this is Lima's natural "air-conditioning." A prevailing southwest wind first strikes the cold Humboldt current of the Pacific Ocean, on which Lima is located. The air passing over this water is chilled before fanning over the land.

One of the city's big showplaces is the Plaza de Armas.* Some well-traveled visitors have called it the most beautiful public square to be found on the American continents. Located on this square is the Roman Catholic archbishop's palace and the city's ancient cathedral. In this cathedral Carlos has seen the displayed remains of the conquistador, Francisco Pizarro, who founded the city in 1535.

Lima was the heart of Spanish power, the capital of Spain's vast holdings in South America for more than two centuries. Its churches and monasteries glittered with gold and silver from Peru's mines. But while Spanish influence spread throughout Latin America, many scattered Indian tribes remained untouched by the new conquerors and their ways.

More than one third of Peru's 19.5 million people live in cities and towns along the coast, while just over one half million live in villages scattered in the jungle east of the Andes. This land, called the Montaña*, borders on the Amazonia of Brazil. Like the people of

150

*Thatched floating houses line shores of Peru's Montaña.
In dry season, rafts rest on river bottom. When rains
come, they rise with waters as far as tether will allow.*

Amazonia, many who live in the Montaña are just beginning to feel the effects of modern times.

Edi* is a 15-year-old girl who lives in the Montaña
in a little Indian village which has no name. Like
João's village in Brazil, it lies on the banks of a river
which flows into the Amazon.

Edi's house, like others in the village, is built on
posts five feet above the ground. These houses on
stilts are designed to remain undisturbed when the
river rises and floods the land around them.

The floor of the house is made of palm logs, and
the roof is thatched with palm leaves. Cooking is done
on a "sand table" on the floor. At night the family
spreads a big cloth on the floor and sleeps upon it.

Edi's family also has a garden, which grows bananas, corn, potatoes, sugar cane, pineapples, and wa-

151

termelons. But much of Edi's food is not grown. It comes straight from the jungle. Hunters still use blowguns to shoot darts tipped with a poison. Poison is also used in fishing.

Edi explains how her people use the poison, which they get from a plant. "We crush the root and mix it with water. Then we spread it on the stream. The poison slows down the fish, and the men kill them with long spears."

Edi's father is a lumberman. He cuts down big trees and makes them into rafts. These he floats down the river to Iquitos*, the largest city in the upper Amazon valley. A round trip takes more than a month.

Though deep in the jungle, where temperatures often soar to above 100 degrees, Iquitos is a bustling regional capital. The story behind the birth, decline, and rebirth of Iquitos is a strange one. It's the story of Amazon rubber and fortunes made and lost.

Early in the 20th century, fortune hunters pushed deep into the Amazon jungles in search of rubber trees. There was a tremendous demand for rubber to make tires for the new "horseless carriages" that were fast gaining popularity in the U.S. and Europe. That demand created an Amazon "gold rush."

But the rush died. An Englishman managed to smuggle a number of rubber tree seedlings out of Brazil. They were planted halfway round the world, in Ceylon (modern Sri Lanka). In time, mature rubber trees in Asia were producing finer and cheaper rubber than could be found in Amazonia.

Cities like Iquitos began declining. Today, however, the people here are making a slow comeback—thanks to some unusual world markets. Instead of selling rubber-tree juice, men from nearby villages are selling monkeys. The city exports about 50,000 live monkeys a year for zoos and laboratories. Another relatively new

152

In the Montaña, a book is a strange and unfamiliar object. These girls, of the Shapibo tribe, share one book in their open-walled schoolhouse.

business is tropical fish, sold for overseas aquariums. Iquitos also does a brisk trade in chicle—a sticky substance which is the chief ingredient of chewing gum.

The biggest story in today's Peru, however, is not on the coast or in the jungles. It is in the Andes mountain region, where Indian peasants live much as they did under the Incas. That's where a guerrilla movement that has terrorized much of Peru is based.

The guerrillas, inspired by Chinese Communists, are known as the Shining Path. Their goal is to overturn Peru's democratic government. "This country's society is corrupt," one rebel told a reporter. "Everything must be torn down so we can·build anew."

Since 1980, the Shining Path has carried on a war of murders, bombings, sabotage, and terror that has reached beyond the mountains and into Lima itself. The group has destroyed millions of dollars worth of roads, bridges, and power plants. Savage fighting between the guerrillas and Peru's armed forces has left more than 6,000 people dead.

Many experts worry that the terrorists of the Shining Path are finding new recruits in the poverty stricken shantytowns of Lima. There, the main problem is the nation's long economic depression, which made Peru the second-poorest country in South America. The average income, per person, is just $825 a year. Out of desperation, many poor city dwellers have turned to crime and violence.

What's more, Peru owes $14 billion to foreign banks. Income from its two main exports, copper and oil, has declined. Many Peruvians have turned to an illegal business, producing cocaine, to combat poverty. In just six years, economists say, cocaine has become the country's most profitable export, earning some $500 million a year.

But there is good news for Peruvians, too. In 1980, Peru ended 12 years of military rule. And in 1985, Peru managed to hold successful new elections. It was the first time in 40 years that Peru had two civilian governments in a row.

The new president, Alan García, seems to symbolize a fresh start for his nation. Only 36, he has captured the imagination of Peruvians with his exuberance and self-confidence. He has clamped down on drug smuggling, moved to repair the economy, and pledged new help for the poor.

Double-check

Review

1. The Incas believed that their emperor was descended from what?

2. At the height of their power, the Incas ruled what area?

3. What have experts called the most important archaeological discovery in South America?

4. Why are some houses in Peru built on stilts?

5. What is the main thing that keeps Iquitos alive?

Discussion

1. What do you think of the Inca systems of distributing land based on family size and of distributing food in lean years based on need? How were these systems different from the system of property and goods distribution in the U.S. and most other developed nations? What are some advantages and disadvantages of each system?

2. Were the actions of Pizarro toward Atahualpa and other Incas smart, good, evil, necessary, or typical of conquistadores? Explain your answers.

3. Edi's village in Peru has no name. Do you think this matters to the residents of the village? Why, or why not? When might such small villages be given, or decide to take, names? Who might name such villages — the residents, the Peruvian government, map makers? Should there be a system for naming remote villages? Who should decide? Why?

Activities

1. Committees of students might prepare bulletin board displays and/or oral reports on the Inca empire and Peru, including their art, music, architecture, language, religion, dress, crafts, customs, politics, and economies.

2. From the information in Chapter 16 (and perhaps other sources), some students might role-play the first meeting of Atahualpa with Pizarro and the Spanish priest. Afterward each of the three main characters should try to explain to the rest of the class why he did what he did at that meeting.

3. Some students might pretend to be Carlos or Edi, writing in their diaries about what they think their lives will be like in the next 10 years, and listing their hopes for their own children.

Skills

POPULATION ESTIMATES, 1984
(in millions)

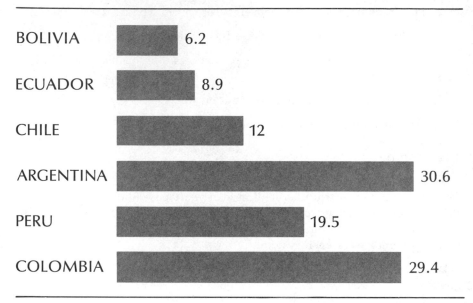

Country	Population
BOLIVIA	6.2
ECUADOR	8.9
CHILE	12
ARGENTINA	30.6
PERU	19.5
COLOMBIA	29.4

Source: Scholastic World Affairs Annual, 1985

Use the bar graph above and information in chapters 16 and 17 to answer the following questions.

1. What do the bars represent?

2. What is the source of information for this graph?

3. How many people were estimated to live in Ecuador in 1984?

4. What country has the largest population?

5. What is the population of the country whose capital attracts about 25,000 new residents each year?

Chapter 18

Ecuador: Two Lives in Contrast

NORTH OF PERU lies the smaller country of Ecuador. Like Peru and Bolivia, it formed part of the vast Inca empire. Today, Ecuador's Inca heritage remains strong. Most of its people are either mestizos or pure Indians.

Many are farmers, who work mainly with hand tools and equipment. Ecuador's main exports are straw hats, bananas, coffee, rice, and cacao* beans. These beans of the cacao tree are the source of all kinds of chocolate.

Ecuador was named for the Equator, which passes almost directly through the country's capital of Quito.* Yet this old city enjoys a moderate year-round average temperature of 70 degrees at noon. The reason is that Quito is nestled 9,350 feet high in the Andes. Since all parts of this small country are near the Equator, the only season is summer.

157

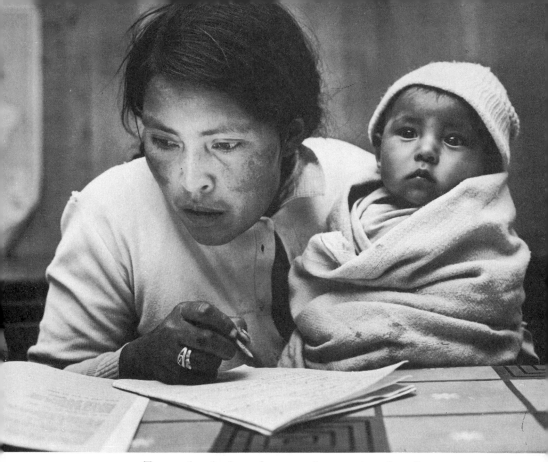

*To people who have known only poverty, education
can bring hope for a better life. Above, a Quecha
woman, baby on her shoulder, learns to write.*

A small group of wealthy landowners, descended
from the Spanish conquistadores, has controlled Ecuador since colonial days. Like most other nations in Latin
America, Ecuador has had its share of military rule.
But, in 1979, it began the current trend toward democracy in the region. That's when its last military junta
peacefully gave way to an elected civilian government.

Rosa, 16, is a member of Ecuador's aristocracy. Her
father has a 500-acre farm about 50 miles north of
Quito. The farm, which is worked by about a dozen
farmhands, produces crops of potatoes and cacao. Rosa
goes to school in the city. However, as soon as her Fri-

day afternoon classes are finished, she rushes home, changes into riding clothes, and leaves for the farm. There she rides her beloved horse, Carmelo. Carmelo, in Spanish, means "caramel candy."

Rosa tells some of the things she likes about farm life: "Our farm is a few miles from the town of Otavalo. The Otavalo Indian tribe lives there. Sunday morning the Indians bring their products to the market place. They sell all kinds of tropical fruits and vegetables. After the market, the Indians dance and play the flute, pan-pipe, guitar, mandolin, a small harp, and drums.

"On the farm we eat different foods than in the city. We often have potato-balls, which we call tortillas. These are different from Mexican tortillas. To make these, you add cheese and butter to mashed potatoes, then you roll it into balls. We fry these in lard and color them with achote* juice. This is a red juice from berries. Indians once used it to paint their bodies."

Rosa is interested in Ecuador's Inca past, though she's of Spanish, not Indian, descent. She and her mother attend auctions and visit Quito's secondhand shops, looking for objects that date back to Inca days. They have a number of water jars that were used by Indians during this time.

☆　☆　☆　☆　☆　☆　☆　☆　☆

Rosa's easy life sounds like a dream to Luisa. She's a 14-year-old Quechua* Indian, born in a tiny village in the Andes.

Luisa was brought up to speak the Quechua language. She speaks Spanish fluently but at home talks only Quechua with her family. Like most Indian languages, Quechua has no alphabet of its own. Long ago the Quechuas "borrowed" the Spanish alphabet.

◆§ Rosa goes to school in the city, but as soon as her Friday afternoon classes are finished, she rushes home, changes into riding clothes, and leaves for the farm.

◆§ Luisa eats her meals outside her house because there is no electricity. She washes dishes by candlelight.

Luisa and her family used to live in a four-room adobe house with whitewashed walls and a tiled roof. The cooking was done on three stones in the middle of the kitchen's earthen floor. A fire was built among the stones, and a cooking pot was placed atop them.

Corn was the main food. The family prepared it every way it knew how: roasted, fried, creamed — Luisa's mother even made a sweet drink of it.

"My mother took care of our little farm plot," Luisa recalls. "That's woman's work among our people. The only thing the men do on the farm is to plow the land before planting."

Five years ago, Luisa's mother took a job as a caretaker at a Catholic school, and the family moved to Quito. The Quechuas don't believe in education for girls, and Luisa didn't begin attending classes until she moved to Quito. She was nine years old when she entered the first grade.

"Now I'm studying physics, chemistry, history, geography, Spanish grammar, art, and singing," she reports. "I have one hour of English a week and two hours of Bible study. For fun the girls play basketball or a hopscotch game that we call *rayola*.* Boys have soccer and volleyball games. Sometimes they play marbles with big seeds."

Life has improved for Luisa since she moved to the city. But most U.S. students would consider her daily routine a hard one.

"I am up at 5:30 to start the wood fire in the school kitchen," Luisa says. "School begins with a chapel service. At nine, we all get a breakfast of some bread and coffee or cocoa. School lasts until 4:30 with nearly two hours for lunch. After school I go home to do my homework and help Mother.

"At six we eat dinner. Mother puts oatmeal, or whatever food she has prepared, into bowls made of gourds. It's dark in the house, so we take our gourds outside to eat. I wash the dishes by candlelight, since we have no electricity. We go to bed at 10."

School offers Luisa and her fellow students a "fringe benefit" — weekly showers. "Once a week, we take showers at school," she says. "Some students keep toothbrushes, combs, and towels at school, because they have no water at home. Sometimes we walk three miles to a public swimming pool."

Luisa would like someday to be a nurse's aide — if she could continue her education. But she doubts that she'll be able to. Still, Luisa is cheerful, squeezing in whatever enjoyment she can.

"We all enjoy fiestas," she says. "The most important day of the year for us is All Souls' Day, which comes in early November. We bake bread in the shape of horses and riders. These are for the boys. The girls get dolls."

Spanish, mestizo, or Indian, rich or poor, Ecuadorian boys and girls are eager to learn, eager to make something of themselves. But an overwhelming number of young people in Ecuador are denied the opportunity for study and advancement.

161

Double-check

Review

1. Most of Ecuador's people are of what two groups?

2. For what geographical feature was Ecuador named?

3. What group has ruled Ecuador since colonial days?

4. How old was Luisa when she entered the first grade?

5. What and when is the most important day of the year for Luisa?

Discussion

1. In what ways are Rosa's and Luisa's lives different? In what ways are they similar? Could they change places successfully? Could they ever be friends? Which person would you rather be? Give reasons for your answers.

2. Rosa and her mother are interested in Ecuador's Inca past. Why do you think they are? Do you think many Spanish Ecuadorians are? Should they be? Are many U.S. citizens interested in their country's Indian past? Are many citizens interested in the Indians who live in their countries today? Do you think the Indians in Ecuador are interested in Spanish culture? Should they be? Explain your answers.

3. Luisa points out that among the Quechua, taking care of the farm plot is women's work, and the Quechuas "don't believe in education for girls." Do you think there is such a thing as men's work and women's work? How is this determined — by the culture? By the men? By the women? Do such beliefs ever change? Should they? Why, or why not?

Activities

1. A committee of students might prepare a bulletin board display and/or oral reports on aspects of life in Ecuador, including the art, music, architecture, language, religion, dress, crafts, customs, politics, and economy.

2. Students might take turns role-playing a meeting between Rosa and Luisa in which each tries to describe her life to the other and they discuss the similarities and differences in their backgrounds.

3. Other students might write short stories in which they tell what happens to Rosa and Luisa during the next 20 years of their lives. Volunteers might read their stories aloud to the rest of the class, who might vote on the story they think is most likely to happen.

Skills

ECUADOR'S ETHNIC AND RELIGIOUS GROUPS

Ethnic Composition   **Religions**

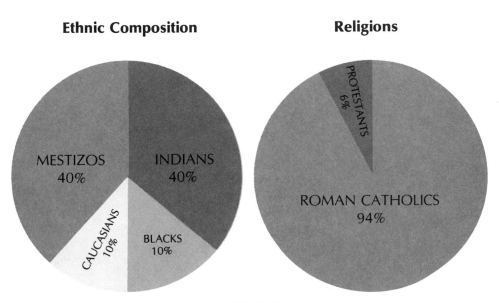

Source: *The 1979 World Almanac*

Use the circle graphs above and information in Chapter 18 to answer the following questions.

1. What does the circle graph on the right represent?

2. What is the source of the information in these graphs?

3. What percentage of Ecuador's people are Protestants?

4. What are the two major ethnic groups in Ecuador?

5. Luisa's people make up what percentage of Ecuador's population?

Chapter 19

Colombia and Bolivia:
The Golden Beggar

In the 16th century men believed there was a place called *El Dorado*, a city of such incredible wealth that it was built entirely of gold. Dreams of finding El Dorado inspired the Spanish conquistadores to great feats of exploration. As long as El Dorado lay just ahead, no climate was too hot, no mountain too rugged, no jungle too forbidding for them.

As far as we know today, El Dorado — "The Golden One" — never existed, except in the fevered minds of men hungering for gold. Yet some of the Spaniards believed that nothing loosened information about gold from an Indian quite as quickly as torture. To avoid such torture, the Indians sometimes spun yarns of great riches — which always lay just over the next mountain.

One such story, however, seems to have been based at least partly on fact. This was the story of the Chibcha* Indians of Colombia.

164

Like most Indians everywhere, the Chibchas had little use for gold except as pure ornament. They had so much that they used it liberally in an annual ceremony. Each year they anointed their chief and rolled him in gold dust. Then the chief would take a ceremonial bath in the sacred lake of the Chibchas to wash away the precious metal.

The Indian tales of gold may have been exaggerated. But plenty of gold was in the New World — and the Spaniards found it.

In 1533 the Spanish founded a port city on the coast of Colombia which was to become one of the most important in the New World. The city was named Cartagena,* after the city of the same name in Spain. Soon, great fleets were stopping at Cartagena to take on gold and other valuables from northern South America to be transported to Spain.

So much gold flowed through Cartagena that it began attracting pirates from all nations. To fend off these buccaneers, Spain began building a huge fortress at Cartagena. Started in 1533 under Philip II, this construction was so gigantic that it was not completed for a hundred years.

One story says that this fortress cost Spain so much money that one day Philip looked through a window of his palace in Madrid trying to see it. He joked that anything that cost so much must be large enough to see — even if it did stand a whole ocean away.

Spain could have saved itself some of the expense. This mighty fortress which towers 135 feet above Cartagena's harbor still is considered a marvel of construction. But it did not hold off the pirates. Despite this great barrier, the city of Cartagena was sacked by such English pirate captains as Henry Morgan and Sir Francis Drake.

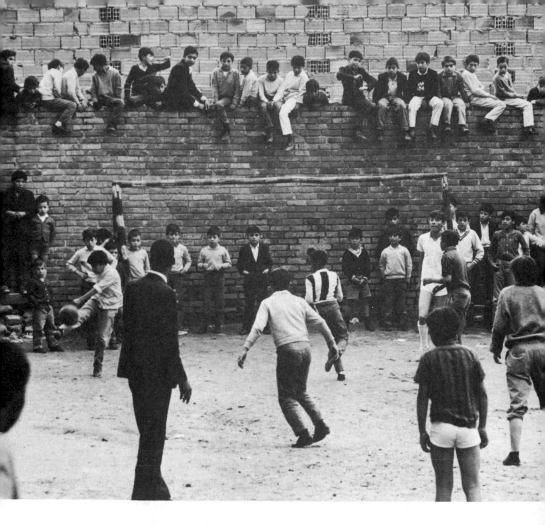

Soccer is as popular in South America as baseball is in the U.S. Above, a pickup game in a vacant lot in Bogotá — with no lack of referees viewing the game from a bird's eye perch.

From Cartagena, Spanish conquistadores fanned out in all directions in search of El Dorado. One of them, Gonzalo Jimínez de Quesada,* led an army along the Magdalena River into the heart of Colombia in 1536. Jimínez de Quesada was determined to match the feats of Cortés in Mexico and Pizarro in Peru. He wasn't easily discouraged.

Shortly after his trip up the river began, several of

166

his rafts overturned, spilling many of the men into the water. About half the army drowned. Jimínez de Quesada pushed on.

He and his men fought the Chibchas and climbed the Andes. On a high plateau protected from wind by surrounding mountain peaks, Jimínez de Quesada founded a city, which he named Santa Fé de Bogotá.* Santa Fé was the name of the explorer's hometown in Spain. To this he added "de Bogotá," the Chibchas' name for the region. Jimínez de Quesada's new name for the city didn't stick. "Santa Fé" was dropped, and his city became known by the name the Indians had for the place all along — Bogotá.

From the start, Bogotá was a wealthy city. Rich hacienda owners imported some of Spain's finest architects and builders. Their workmanship can still be seen in the city's old churches and magnificent homes. Four-lane highways run beside narrow streets laid out in colonial days. Steel and glass skyscrapers soar into the air beside one-story shacks. Everywhere there are beautiful gardens.

Yet Colombia is a nation which, like Ecuador and Peru, has remained isolated from the world. Few foreigners have settled here. As a result, the language and manners of the early Spanish settlers have been preserved in parts of Colombia. For this reason, some people say that Colombia is "more Spanish than Spain." Spanish visitors, for example, are delighted to hear expressions in Bogotá that long ago were abandoned in the "old country." Courtly old men in Bogotá address each other as *"Su Merced"* — "Your Mercy."

But Colombia's Indian heritage is seen on the streets of Bogotá, too. Visiting village women wear long skirts, rope-soled shoes, shawls, and braided hair — as Indian women have worn for generations.

167

Indian men wear white trousers that reach just below their knees, blanket-like capes, and straw hats.

Poverty and isolation are reasons that both Bolivia and Colombia have become leading producers of a profitable but deadly crop. That crop is cocaine, produced from the coca leaves which grow in the region.

Traditionally, the area's poor Indians have chewed coca leaves to relieve their hunger. But in recent years, criminal groups have set up huge illegal operations to produce cocaine for export to U.S. drug-abusers. Despite pressure from the U.S. to stop these drug producers, many operate openly, protected by private armies and payoffs to government officials.

Bolivia was also part of the Inca empire. In 1545 a great discovery was made at Cerro Rico Mountain — silver. This precious metal was so plentiful that it seemed the whole mountain might be made of it.

As usual, few persons in Bolivia benefited from the country's wealth. Spain set up a mint near Cerro Rico and turned the metal into coins right on the spot. Almost all the coins were shipped to Spain — if they got by the pirates!

Indians who worked the mines lived and labored under inhuman conditions. The country was once described as "a beggar sitting on a chair of gold." That description is not quite accurate. The last word should have been "silver."

Bolivia is still chiefly a mining state. But now the metal on which it mainly depends is not silver. It's tin. This country shares the problems that plague most of its neighbors, plus a few special ones of its own. One of the biggest of these is that Bolivia is landlocked. Surrounded by five countries — Brazil, Paraguay, Argentina, Chile, and Peru — Bolivia has no direct access to the ocean. The cost of transporting

*Against the barren backdrop of the
Colombian Andes, descendants of the Chibcha
Indians carry a simple wooden coffin to
its final resting place in the earth.*

products such as its tin over the rugged mountains is high.

Progress in Bolivia has been an uphill battle. Almost two thirds of its estimated six million people live outside the cities, most of them in the mountainous west. About 60 per cent of the people are Indians, set in their ways. Most of the others are mestizos.

169

Simón Bolívar played an historic role in South American history by freeing the land of the Incas from Spanish rule.

"THE LIBERATOR"

THE MAN WHO played the biggest part in driving the Spaniards from much of South America was Simón Bolívar, known as "The Liberator." Born in 1783 in what is now Venezuela, he spent much of his life freeing Colombia, Ecuador, and Peru as well as his native country from Spanish domination.

Bolívar's father, a Creole aristocrat of Caracas, died when Simón was three. Young Bolívar's mother died six years later. The youth was cared for by an uncle. At 16 he was sent to Europe to complete his education. For three years he lived in Spain. There he married the daughter of a Spanish nobleman. Less than a year after the marriage, his bride died of yellow fever.

In 1811 Bolívar became a lieutenant of Francisco Miranda, a revolutionary leader. Miranda was soon captured and spent the rest of his life in Spanish dungeons. Bolívar fled to Colombia, then known as New Grenada, to continue his fight against Spanish tyranny.

The people of Cartagena rallied around Bolívar and named him commander of a force to liberate Venezuela. Bolívar was defeated several times. He barely missed being captured by Spanish troops. Three years after he had departed on his hopeful mission, he returned to Cartagena, his dream unrealized.

Bolívar didn't lose faith in that dream — and neither did the people of Cartagena. Bolívar managed to reinforce his small army with several hundred foreign soldiers, most of them British and Irish. Then he hit on one of the boldest military plans ever carried out.

Bogotá was an important city firmly in the hands of Spanish forces. To drive the Spaniards from there, Bolívar decided that his army of about 2,500 men would have to catch them by surprise. He would do this by leading his men through the Andes Mountains.

There was one pass, high in the remote mountains, to the plains surrounding Bogotá. But it was rugged terrain, buffeted by icy winds. It seemed impossible to the Spaniards that an invading force could possibly travel across it.

To reach the pass, Bolívar's men had to make their way across barren, windswept plains. It was the rainy season. For a week the men trudged through mud, sometimes wading through water up to their waists.

When they reached the Andes, the soldiers realized that things so far had been easy compared to what lay ahead. They were lightly dressed. Many froze or died of exposure while crossing the mountains. At last the remnants of Bolívar's tattered forces descended onto the plains around Bogotá.

The Spanish were so surprised by Bolívar's troops they couldn't get organized. The Spanish were defeated in battle, and the major part of the royalist army surrendered. When Bolívar entered Bogotá three days later, it was the beginning of the end of Spanish rule in the land of the Incas.

Bolívar dreamed of a league of Latin American states to bring cooperation between nations. But he was ahead of his time. It wasn't until almost a hundred years later that an effective organization was formed along the lines he proposed.

Bolívar was saddened by the strife which broke out among the new nations after the defeat of the Spaniards. Before he died of tuberculosis on December 17, 1830, he wrote bitterly of his life's work: "We've ploughed the sea." By this he meant that trying to unite Latin America was as impossible a job as trying to plough the sea.

But history doesn't share that opinion. Bolívar has become a towering symbol of Latin American freedom.

Double-check

Review

1. What was El Dorado?

2. How did the Indians avoid torture from the Spaniards?

3. What great discovery was made in 1545 at Cerro Rico Mountain?

4. How did Bolívar spend much of his life?

5. What did Bolívar dream of for Latin America?

Discussion

1. Spanish conquistadores were inspired to great feats of exploration in search of gold. Do you think much of Latin America would have been explored without this motivation? Why, or why not? What else might motivate people to explore unknown regions?

2. One of the major problems for Bolivian commerce is that the country is landlocked. What other Latin American country is similarly situated? What are some other disadvantages of being landlocked? What might be some advantages? How might each country overcome this problem?

3. Why do you think it was important to Bolívar to try to unite Latin America? Why do you think it was so difficult? Do you agree with his assessment that it was an impossible dream at that time? Was Bolívar's work a failure? What might be some reasons for Latin American countries to unite? What are some arguments against uniting?

Activities

1. Committees of students might prepare bulletin board displays and/or oral reports on aspects of life in Colombia and Bolivia, including art, music, architecture, language, religion, dress, crafts, customs, politics, and economies.

2. Some students might pretend to be TV reporters interviewing other students pretending to be members of Bolívar's army. The soldiers could try to explain what the long march was like, why they fought with Bolívar against the Spanish, and what they hope for in the future.

3. The Organization of American States (OAS) was formed in Bogotá, Colombia, in 1948. There are 28 member-nations, including the U.S. Some students might research and report on this organization's activities.

Skills

Bolivia

Colombia

A. The Chibcha Indians lived there.

B. De Quesada founded a city there.

C. Silver was discovered there in 1545.

D. It is landlocked.

E. Cartagena is located there.

F. It depends mostly on tin.

G. A fortress there failed to hold off pirates.

H. It was once described as "a beggar sitting on a chair of gold."

I. It is said to be "more Spanish than Spain."

J. About 60 per cent of its people are Indians.

K. Its Indian village women wear native dress.

Use the list above and information in Chapter 19 to do the following things on a separate sheet of paper.

1. Write the letters given above down the left side of the paper.

2. Using information in the chapter, write either "Colombia," "Bolivia," or "Colombia and Bolivia" next to the letter of each sentence, telling which country the sentence describes. (Some sentences describe *both* countries.)

Chapter 20

Venezuela:
Country of "Black Gold"

IRIS, A GIRL of Caracas,* is a busy young teenager. She's up early to go to school. She goes home to lunch at 11. Lunch is the big meal of the day in Iris' house. The noon meal may be a steak with a spicy sauce or chicken cooked with rice. Iris' classes resume at two and last until four.

Like many girls her age in the United States, Iris plays volleyball and basketball during her gym classes. She studies Spanish grammar, literature and composition, history and geography, arithmetic, health, and music appreciation. She has about three hours of homework each night.

When she gets a chance, she listens to rock. But when she sits at the piano, she plays classical music. Besides music lessons, Iris takes lessons in English. She's a girl of many interests. Her favorite is travel.

Her father, a ladies' clothing manufacturer, used to take his family on his business trips to the United

ᵉᵍ Venezuela is one of the richest countries in South America. But it has only one big "crop" — oil.

States. "We may not be making so many business trips now," says Iris. "Father used to buy his textiles in the United States. But he says that in the last few years he has been able to buy many materials here in Venezuela."

When a girl Iris' age hears the phrase "changing economy," it usually means little. But Iris can understand why she no longer will be traveling so much. And the reason for this — the fact that Venezuela is now producing things it once did not — is a sign of that country's changing economy.

Venezuela is one of the richest countries in South America. It hasn't always been rich, although much of its history has been associated with treasure-seekers.

When Columbus made his third voyage to the New World, he landed on the mainland of South America and reported seeing Indians wearing rich ornaments of pearls and gold. Just how true this was is anybody's guess. Columbus wasn't always a very accurate reporter. To convince his patrons in Europe to send him on new voyages, he sometimes let his imagination run wild.

Columbus' story touched off yet another search for the fabled land of El Dorado. No one ever found it, but the searchers did give Venezuela its name. When one explorer saw a group of Indian huts built atop piles in the waters of Lake Maracaibo,* the scene reminded him of Venice. He called the place Venezuela — "Little Venice."

For centuries Venezuela was regarded as backward. Then, in 1918, an expedition searching the area around Lake Maracaibo discovered something in the water as valuable as gold. They found a special kind of gold — "black gold." Oil.

Ramón,* a 15-year-old boy, tells what it's like to live near the source of so much of Venezuela's wealth. "I live near one of the richest oil fields in the world — Lake Maracaibo," he says.

"Standing in the waters of the lake are the oil derricks. They pump up oil from the bottom of the lake. The derricks look like a forest of pine trees growing right out of the water" (see photo essay, page 101).

"Along the edges of the lake are huts that stand on stilts in the shallow water. Indians have built these huts for hundreds of years. Before the Spaniards came, Indians used the sticky black asphalt that they found near the lake. They'd put some on the end of a stick and light it for a torch. Or they'd smear the asphalt on their canoes to make them watertight." Asphalt, a form of petroleum, is a sign that a pool of oil is nearby.

Ramón was born in the city of Maracaibo, on the northwest tip of the lake. Now he lives on the lake's east side in the town of Cabimas. The family moved because their new home is closer to the machine shop where Ramón's father works. He's a mechanic for one of the companies which has an agreement with the government to drill for oil in the lake. Ramón goes to a private school which the company built for the children of its workers.

Soon after oil was discovered near where Ramón now lives, Venezuela began exporting huge quantities of petroleum. The national income rose rapidly, but the new wealth was held by a favored few. After years of rule by dictators who came from these favored few, Venezuelans had had enough. In 1958

177

they revolted and, with the help of the army, established democratic government in Venezuela.

After 1958 Venezuela underwent a democratic revolution that helped benefit the poor. New schools were built. School attendance doubled. Adults who had never learned were taught to read. Within a few years Venezuela's literacy rate of 50 percent was greatly improved. Today, only 12 percent of its adults cannot read, one of the lowest rates in Latin America.

As elsewhere in Latin America, most of Venezuela's fertile land was owned by a few old families. A new program began breaking up these big holdings and granted land to more than 60,000 families.

Agriculture is still a big problem in this country, which has only one big "crop" — oil. (Petroleum accounts for more than 80 per cent of Venezuela's exports.) The big trouble is that there's not enough land under cultivation to grow enough food for Venezuela's people.

Only two per cent of Venezuela's total area consists of farmland. Dense forests cover about one fourth of the nation. Rugged Andes Mountain terrain takes up another big part. What's left, beside the farmlands around Lake Maracaibo and Lake Valencia, is mostly a plain which is either too wet or too dry to farm most of the year.

In recent years, the Venezuelan government has been aiding farmers by installing irrigation projects. It has also lent the farmers money so they can buy better fertilizers and new farm machinery. But so far, oil-rich Venezuela still has to import a more common liquid — milk. It also depends on other countries for large quantities of meat.

Venezuela's dependence on oil hurt it in the mid-1980's. About half of the government's money comes from taxes levied on the oil industry. When oil prices dropped, the economy slowed and the government ran up big debts.

Like people through much of Latin America, the poor people of Caracas try to forget their troubles at the fiestas. One game they play seems especially appropriate for Latin Americans. The boys try to climb a pole slicked with grease. There's a sack of money and toys on top of the pole which is theirs — if they can just climb the pole to get it.

In many ways, Venezuela is playing the same frustrating game. The way to the top of the pole is long and difficult, and the player who stops to rest may find himself sliding down to the bottom. With its fast-growing population and dependence on one "crop" — in this case, its oil industry exports — Venezuela is not much different from a number of other Latin American countries. With a tremendous effort, it has managed to pull itself close to the top of the pole in the past two decades. But if it stops to rest, it may find itself sliding back down the greased pole into all the troubles that beset much of the rest of Latin America.

Double-check

Review

1. What is a sign of Venezuela's changing economy?

2. What does the name *Venezuela* mean?

3. What is a sign that a pool of oil is nearby?

4. What percentage of Venezuela's total area is farmland?

5. Venezuela's economy seems dangerously balanced on the shoulders of what one "strong man"?

Discussion

1. Venezuela's economy changed rapidly with the discovery of oil. What aspects of a nation's social and cultural life might be affected by a rapid rise in national income levels? How would these aspects of life be affected by a drop in income levels?

2. Do you think the Venezuelan government's actions in breaking up large landholdings and giving the land to 60,000 families were fair and wise? What arguments might be made for such land reform? What arguments might be made against it?

3. This chapter points out, "Like people through much of Latin America, the poor people of Caracas try to forget their troubles at the fiestas." Do you think this is good, bad, necessary, or unimportant? What other purposes do such fiestas serve — for individuals and for their nation as a whole?

Activities

1. A committee of students might prepare a bulletin board display and/or oral reports on aspects of life in Venezuela, including art, music, architecture, language, dress, religion, crafts, customs, politics, and the economy.

2. Some students might draw political cartoons illustrating one or more of the following: the importance of oil to the Venezuelan economy; the importance of fiestas in the life of the nation; Venezuela's efforts to pull itself up the greased pole of success; the effects of land reform on different families; Venezuela's need to import food.

3. Several students might role-play a meeting of a committee of Venezuelan leaders responsible for planning their nation's economic and social development during the next 20 years.

Skills

SECONDARY SCHOOL TEACHERS AND STUDENTS
1983
(in thousands)

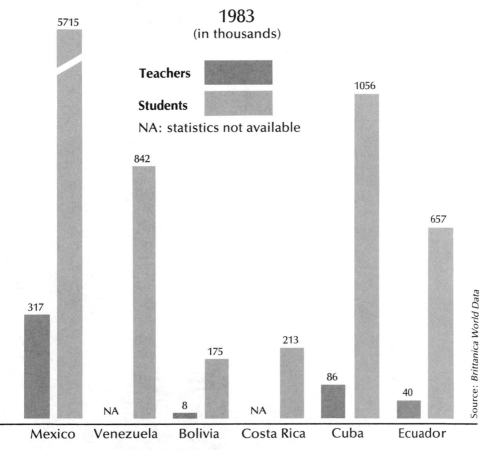

Teachers (dark)

Students (light)

NA: statistics not available

Source: Brittanica World Data

| Mexico | Venezuela | Bolivia | Costa Rica | Cuba | Ecuador |

- Mexico: 5715, 317
- Venezuela: 842, NA
- Bolivia: 175, 8
- Costa Rica: 213, NA
- Cuba: 1056, 86
- Ecuador: 657, 40

Use the bar graph above and information in Chapter 20 to answer the following questions.

1. What do the light bars represent? The dark bars?

2. Which country had the most students in secondary schools in 1983? Which country had the fewest?

3. How many Bolivian secondary school students were there for each teacher in 1983?

4. Iris is one of how many secondary school students in her country?

5. In which country are teachers likely to have the smallest classes?

5
CENTRAL AMERICA AND THE CARIBBEAN

Chapter 21

Panama and the Canal

IN 1502 COLUMBUS sailed the ocean blue to within a few miles of the route to the Indies for which he had long been searching.

As his ships made their way along the coast of Central America, Columbus came as close to his goal as he ever would. For, although he did not know it, across this narrow neck of land (*isthmus*) lay the Pacific Ocean, and beyond it Asia. Columbus never saw the Pacific. Indeed, he had little reason to suspect its existence. For all he knew, the land stretched westward for thousands of miles.

Columbus kept skirting the coastline, looking for a wide river through or a passageway around this big "island." Finally, on Easter night 1503, he set sail for Spain "with the ships rotten, worm-eaten, all in holes." It was his fourth and last expedition to the New World.

Spaniards didn't learn what was on the other side of the isthmus until 10 years later. Then Vasco Nuñez de Balboa,* leading 190 Spaniards and 800 Indians from Darien in Panama, marched inland to find out. After a journey of four weeks, he reached a body of water which he called "the South Sea." It came to be known as the Pacific Ocean.

To reach the Pacific by land, Balboa would have journeyed only about 40 miles from the Caribbean coast — if he had gone in a straight line. But to reach the Pacific by ship Ferdinand Magellan in 1520 had to sail around the South American continent.

What this new route to the Indies needed was a canal. It would cut the voyage between Europe and Asia by thousands of miles. But the canal remained a dream for almost 400 years. During those centuries ships followed Magellan's long route around South America through the strait named for him.

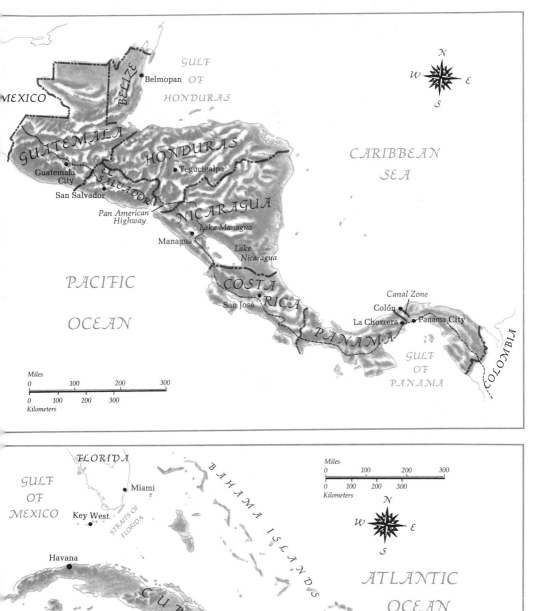

GULF OF HONDURAS

MEXICO

BELIZE

Belmopan

GUATEMALA

Guatemala City

San Salvador

EL SALVADOR

HONDURAS

Tegucigalpa

Pan American Highway

NICARAGUA

Lake Managua

Managua

Lake Nicaragua

CARIBBEAN SEA

PACIFIC OCEAN

COSTA RICA

San José

PANAMA

Canal Zone

Colón

La Chorrera

Panama City

GULF OF PANAMA

COLOMBIA

N
W E
S

Miles
0   100   200   300

0   100   200   300
Kilometers

FLORIDA

GULF OF MEXICO

Miami

Key West

STRAITS OF FLORIDA

BAHAMA ISLANDS

Miles
0   100   200   300

0   100   200   300
Kilometers

N
W E
S

Havana

ISLE OF PINES

CUBA

ORIENTE

SIERRA MAESTRA MTS.

Guantánamo Bay

U.S. Naval Base

JAMAICA

Kingston

ATLANTIC OCEAN

HISPANIOLA

HAITI

Port-au-Prince

DOMINICAN REPUBLIC

Santo Domingo

San Juan

PUERTO RICO
(U.S.)

CARIBBEAN SEA

❧ From the beginning, the canal has dominated Panama's life. It attracts ships of all nations and has made Panama a "crossroad of the world."

In the mid-1800's, Panama — then part of Colombia — became tremendously important because of its special location between two oceans. Gold had been discovered in California; and in 1849 the Gold Rush was on. People from all over the world began flocking to California to strike it rich.

The overland route across the United States meant a rough journey by covered wagon. A much easier way to get to California was to go by Panama. A U.S. company built a railroad across the narrow isthmus of Panama in 1855. People arriving by ship on Panama's Caribbean coast took a train across Panama. From the city of Panama they boarded a northbound ship up the Pacific coast to California.

The success of this railroad rekindled the old dream of a canal across Panama, the narrowest strip of land between the Atlantic and Pacific. The job of trying to turn that dream into reality was first undertaken by a French company, led by Ferdinand de Lesseps, builder of the Suez Canal. After 10 years of digging, the French company went bankrupt in 1889.

The United States then began trying to reach an agreement with Colombia to build such a canal. Before it spent millions of dollars on this project, however, the United States demanded assurance that it would be able to keep control of the canal after it was built.

After long negotiations, diplomats wrote a treaty to give the United States this right. The people of the region were delighted. They knew that the canal would bring jobs and money. Then, in August 1903, the Colombian senate surprised almost everybody by rejecting the treaty.

Many Panamanians had long been unhappy with rule from Bogotá. The rejection of the canal treaty was the final straw. With ample encouragement and aid from the U.S., the Panamanians rose in revolt.

On November 6, 1903, the United States recognized the new Republic of Panama three days after it declared its independence. From this new nation it leased a 10-mile-wide strip of land and began one of the world's most remarkable engineering feats. The canal was completed in 1914.

From the beginning, the canal has dominated Panama's life. The canal attracts ships of all nations and has made Panama "a crossroad of the world." Colón and Panama City, at opposite ends of the "big ditch," are busy cities which show many foreign influences. Their bustling shops have an international array of merchandise.

A little way outside the cities, however, Spanish colonial culture mixes with that of the Indians. There are Indian villages where people still speak only their native Indian tongue. Many people still wear Indian dress. Their religion, although Catholic, may also include some of the ancient gods the tribe was worshipping before Columbus.

☆　☆　☆　☆　☆　☆　☆　☆　☆

Josefina* is a 14-year-old girl who was born in Panama City. "I think people in Panama are friendlier than in the U.S.," she says. "The friendliest people of all are those of La Chorrera. This is the small town near my grandparents' farm. People there say 'hello' when they meet you on the street, whether they know you or not.

"On the farm we have lots of fun. We ride horses and help take care of the animals. My grandparents raise chickens and have a flock of 75 sheep. Grandmother's hobby is raising rabbits, which are very good to eat.

"I have my own flower garden to take care of, go exploring in the forests nearby, and wade in the river. I love animals and I'd like to be a veterinarian, but I can't hurt them — not even to help them. So I may be a pharmacist instead."

College-bound girls like Josefina aren't as rare in Panama as they are elsewhere in Latin America. Panama gives high priority to education. The government spends more money on education than it does on any other single item in its budget.

One reason Panama can spend so much for education is the canal, which is responsible for much of Panama's prosperity. Sailors and tourists from ships passing through the canal spend much money in Panama's shops. And the canal itself provides jobs for many Panamanians.

Yet Panama has depended on the canal for its livelihood so much that it has failed to develop its own economy. It must buy many of its necessities from foreign countries. It exports only such products as bananas, sugar, coffee, and hardwood.

In 1977 the United States and Panama agreed to treaties that arranged for Panama to take control of the canal gradually, and for U.S. troops to withdraw. The U.S. Senate ratified the treaties in 1978. When Panama took over the Canal Zone in 1979, its president, Aristides Royo, said: "Respect, security, and fraternity between our peoples will be the tonic upon new relations, because the U.S. and Panama have begun a new era in their ties."

Double-check

Review

1. Why did Panama — then a part of Colombia — become tremendously important in the mid-1800's?

2. Before the United States spent millions of dollars on a canal across Panama, what did it demand?

3. When was the canal completed?

4. On what item does the Panamanian government spend more money than on any other single item in its budget?

5. Panama has depended on the canal so much for its livelihood that what has happened?

Discussion

1. Do you think the U.S. had the right to encourage and aid the 1903 Panamanian revolt against the Colombian government? Should the U.S. still do such things when it's in its own self-interest? Why, or why not?

2. Do you think the U.S. was right to demand control of the canal after it was built? What other arrangements for control might have been made? Give reasons for your answers.

3. This chapter points out that the Panamanian government "spends more money on education than it does on any other single item in its budget." Why do you think they do this? What are some advantages of such budgetary priorities? What might be some disadvantages? Should *all* governments do the same with their money? Why, or why not?

Activities

1. A committee of students might prepare a bulletin board display and/or oral reports of various aspects of life in Panama, including art, music, architecture, language, religion, dress, crafts, customs, politics, and the economy.

2. Some students might pretend to be editors of Colombian newspapers in 1903 and write editorials for or against the canal treaty proposed by the U.S. at that time. Other students might draw political cartoons illustrating the Colombian or the U.S. point of view.

3. Two small groups of students might research the controversy that took place in the late 1970's over control of the canal. Then they could hold an informal debate in front of the rest of the class, arguing for and against the 1978 canal treaty.

Skills

ROOSEVELT AND THE CANAL

The Panama Canal I naturally take special interest in because I started it. . . . The Panama Canal would not have been started if I had not taken hold of it, because if I had followed the traditional or conservative method I should have submitted an admirable state paper occupying a couple of hundred pages detailing all the facts to Congress and asking Congress' consideration of it.

In that case there would have been a number of excellent speeches made on the subject in Congress; the debate would be proceeding at this moment with great spirit and the beginning of work on the canal would be 50 years in the future. [Laughter and applause.]

Fortunately . . . I could act unhampered. Accordingly I . . . started the canal and then left Congress not to debate the canal, but to debate me. [Laughter and applause.]

— Theodore Roosevelt speech,
March 23, 1911

Use the above passage and information in Chapter 21 to answer the following questions.

1. From what is the passage above excerpted?

2. What does the information within the brackets represent?

3. What is Roosevelt's attitude in the passage?

4. What seems to be the main point of the passage?

5. This passage dates from how many years before the completion of the Panama Canal?

Chapter 22

Central America:
Shaky Foundations

IN THE 1980'S, no region of Latin America has worried its U.S. friend more than the seven countries of Central America.

The reason for worry about this bridge of land that lies between Mexico and South America is simple. Central America is a region at war with itself. Civil wars continue to ravage three of the region's countries—El Salvador, Guatemala, and Nicaragua. These struggles have claimed more than 150,000 lives since 1979. And the neighboring countries of Costa Rica and Honduras fear that war will spill across their borders.

The violence that plagues most Central Americans, experts say, is the result of generations of poverty, repression, and official corruption. For decades, most Central American countries were ruled by a tiny elite. The elite was usually protected and supported by the military. In El Salvador, for example, 14 families owned 60 percent of the land. Up to one fourth of the population was employed as migratory farm workers—when it was employed at all.

Similar conditions existed throughout the region. Then, in the 1960's and 1970's, small rebel armies formed to fight for change. Some of these rebel groups turned to Communist nations, such as Cuba and the Soviet Union, for aid and arms. But government forces fought back. For the average Central American, life has been unpredictable. Year after year of strife has disrupted businesses, halted development, and broken up families.

Ligia Garcia knows about civil war first-hand. Ligia, 15, lives in Estili, a city of 60,000 in northern Nicaragua. Her oldest brother, Wilfredo, was killed during Nicaragua's revolution in 1979. He had joined the Sandinistas*, the guerrilla fighters who led the uprising against Anastasio Somoza. Somoza was a dictator whose family had ruled Nicaragua since 1933. The Somoza family owned 8,260 square miles of Nicaragua, and businesses worth $500 million. Somoza fled the country after he was driven from power. He was later assassinated in Paraguay.

The Sandinistas named themselves after an earlier guerrilla leader, General Cesar Sandino. In 1912, U.S. Marines were rushed to Nicaragua to protect U.S.-owned businesses. The Marines stayed almost continuously until 1933. Beginning in 1927, however, General Sandino's guerrillas tried to drive out the Marines. Before the Marines pulled out, they trained Nicaragua's army and named Somoza's father as its leader. Sandino was killed on Somoza's orders.

Many Nicaraguans feel that the Somoza government was bad, and that change was needed. Ligia, for one, agrees. "Before," she says, "only the rich kids could go to school and participate in competitions. Now," she

192

says, pointing to a medal she won in a shotput contest, "everyone can participate."

After high school, Ligia wants to study biology at a university. But Nicaragua's schools are overcrowded and poorly supplied. Sometimes as many as 10 students must share a single book. Every morning, Ligia and other students work at the community garden, where the school grows vegetables and wheat. From December through March, during harvest time, they pick cotton and coffee on farms outside of town. "We do anything the revolution asks us," says Ligia. "We do whatever is necessary to keep our liberty."

But not all Nicaraguans feel free. The Sandinista leaders are Marxists, who believe that the government should control the economy—along with most other parts of the nation's life. Neighborhood committees keep track of the government's critics. More than 1,400 Nicaraguans who disagree with the Sandinistas have been jailed. The newspapers, TV, and radio are censored. Many critics of the new government have joined the contras, rebel groups that are trying to overthrow the Sandinistas. Their goal is to set up a democratic government and remove government controls from the nation's economy. The contra efforts, backed by the U.S., has taken a heavy toll on Nicaragua's economy and morale. More than 40 percent of the nation's budget pays for defense. With 50,000 regular troops and 50,000 militia, Nicaragua has Central America's largest armed force. All men between the ages of 17 and 40 must join the army.

Elsewhere in Central America, regional experts point to a few hopeful signs. In El Salvador, the election of President José Napoleón Duarte in 1984 put an end to several decades of harsh military rule. But rebel groups still hope to topple the government. Duarte, a moderate with close ties to the U.S., has tried to negotiate with

Most Central American countries base their
economies on the export of one or two
crops. Here Guatemalan bananas are being
loaded by conveyor for shipment overseas.

rebel leaders. He has also clamped down on the "death squads." These are groups of thugs who use murder and violence against civilians to oppose change.

The United Fruit Company plays an especially important role in Guatemala as well as in several other Central American countries. These countries produce next to nothing for the world market except fruit. There are many Central Americans who hate the influence United Fruit has in their country. They say that it makes fat profits off the labor of the poverty-stricken Indians. But there are others who say that United Fruit has helped raise the standard of living of its workers. These workers, they say, no longer fear hunger. The same cannot be said of other, less fortunate people in most of Central America.

Costa Rica is a happy exception to the story of most Central American countries. Its name in Spanish means "Rich Coast." And, though its people aren't all rich, they are lucky on several counts.

Costa Ricans have lived under democracy during most of the country's life as a republic. Costa Ricans are proud that they have more teachers than soldiers. And a surprisingly large number of peasants own their own land. They grow coffee, cacao, bananas, and hemp.

Double-check

Review

1. What is the main problem of most Central Americans?

2. Traditionally, who controlled most of the land in Central American countries?

3. What do experts say are the causes of the current violence?

4. Besides Nicaragua, what other Central American nations are disruprted by civil war?

5. Costa Ricans have lived under what type of government during most of the country's life as a republic?

Discussion

1. What do you think it would be like to live in a country during a civil war? Would it be better to try to leave the country or to fight for the side you support? Who usually suffers the most in such situations? Who usually gains the most? Explain your answers.

2. Are there major advantages or disadvantages in having most of a nation's land controlled by a small number of people? If such a situation should be changed, what is the best way to work out the changes? Can violence be avoided?

3. When Anastasio Somoza was forced out of Nicaragua in 1979, he came to the U.S. to spend his last years, but he soon left, after much controversy over his being in this country. Should the U.S. allow overthrown rulers to live here? Why, or why not?

Activities

1. Committees of students might prepare a bulletin board display and/or oral reports on various aspects of life in Central American nations, such as the art, music, religion, architecture, language, dress, crafts, customs, politics, and economies.

2. Several students might role-play a discussion between Ligia and her friends about whether she should become a scientist or a biology teacher in Estili.

3. Some students might write short stories in which they tell what happens to Ligia and her nation during the next 20 years. Volunteers might read their stories to the rest of the class.

Skills

STANDARDS OF LIVING IN CENTRAL AMERICA

Country	TV sets per 1000 people	Citizens with safe water	Doctors per 1000 people	Homes with electricity
Costa Rica	72	81%	1.6	71%
El Salvador	62	48%	1.5	34%
Guatemala	24	42%	2.8	29%
Honduras	13	55%	1.2	25%
Nicaragua	65	46%	1.2	41%

Source: *World Military and Social Expenditures, 1983*

Use the table above and information in Chapter 22 to answer the following questions.

1. Which country has the most doctors per 1000 people?

2. If there were 10,000 people in a city in Honduras, how many of them could you expect to have electricity in their homes?

3. What percentage of people in Guatemala do *not* have safe water to drink?

4. If there are 1,000 people in Celestino's town, how many television sets could you expect there to be?

5. In which of these countries would you say the standard of living is highest? Explain.

Chapter 23

Cuba:
Colony to Communist Nation

CHRISTOPHER COLUMBUS discovered Cuba on his first voyage to the New World. It became one of Spain's first footholds on this side of the Atlantic. More recently, when Fidel Castro came to power in 1959, it became the first Communist-controlled country in the Western Hemisphere.

Cuba was almost the last Spanish colony in Latin America to win its independence. An uprising in 1868 took 10 years to put down and cost about 200,000 Cuban and Spanish lives. For years, many in the United States had been interested in driving the Spanish out of Cuba. Then, in 1898, the U.S. battleship *Maine* was mysteriously blown up in Havana's harbor. The U.S. quickly declared war on Spain.

The Spanish-American War lasted only a few months. The U.S. crushed Spain's forces. The peace treaty gave the U.S. control of Cuba and Puerto Rico in the Caribbean, and the Philippines and Guam in the Pacific.

Having no desire to keep Cuba, the U.S. let the island run its own affairs. The U.S. did, however, exert a strong influence over the economy. It also kept control over a large naval base at Guantanamo, on the island's south-eastern shore. During Cuba's first 25 years of independence, the U.S. stepped in several times to stop uprisings.

Like so many other Latin American countries, Cuba suffered through years of rule by military dictators. The last of these was Fulgencio Batista*, who seized power in 1933.

Batista ruled harshly. His secret police tortured many. But the police failed to stop a young lawyer named Fidel Castro. In 1953, Castro led a raid on Batista's army barracks. The raid failed, and Castro was jailed. After his release from jail, Castro organized a new rebel movement. He promised democracy and prosperity to the people, and defeat for Batista.

In 1956, Castro led a well-armed group of revolutionaries to a mountain hideaway. From there, they conducted a widespread campaign of guerrilla warfare. Slowly, the rebels wore down Batista's strength. On New Year's Day, 1959, Batista packed his suitcases full of money and fled the country. Castro marched down from the mountains and entered Havana, the capital, in triumph.

But in less than a year, Castro began to break his promises. He said free elections weren't needed, since he "knew" the Cuban people backed him. Batista's followers and other "enemies of the people" were rounded up and shot by firing squads. By 1961, about 700 had been executed. Thousands of others languished in jail. Many Cubans fled to the U.S., including many of the island's most educated and skilled people.

Castro was soon blaming the U.S. for Cuba's ills. He claimed that U.S. businesses controlled too much of Cu-

Propaganda slogans get a workout in Cuba. This billboard celebrates the defeat of anti-Castro Cubans at the Bay of Pigs in 1961. Beneath it, Cuban school boys do physical exercises.

ba's economy. By the end of 1960, Castro's government had seized about one billion dollars worth of property owned by U.S. businesses and individuals in Cuba. In January 1961, the U.S. broke diplomatic relations with Cuba. A month later, Castro reorganized his government along communist lines and turned to the Soviet Union for support.

Castro's alliance with the Soviet Union set the stage for two dramatic confrontations with the U.S. In April, 1961, about 1,200 Cuban political exiles landed at Cuba's Bay of Pigs in an attempt to overthrow Castro. U.S. intelligence officers, who backed and trained the invaders, had predicted that they would be joined by rebels inside Cuba. But the uprising never occurred, and the invasion was crushed.

A year later, what became known as the Cuban Missile Crisis brought the world dangerously close to nuclear war. The crisis began when U.S. spy planes produced evidence of missile bases under construction in Cuba. The bases were being secretly prepared for Soviet nuclear missiles. U.S. President John F. Kennedy made the evidence public, and demanded that the Soviets remove the missiles. The United States put up a naval blockade, and a tense standoff ended when the Soviets lost their nerve. The missiles were removed before they were targeted at the U.S.

Many of the thousands of Cubans who fled their homeland in the 1960's settled in Miami, Florida. At first, many hoped that Castro could be overthrown and they could return. But as that hope faded, the newcomers settled down to learn English and get jobs. Cuban businesses were soon flourishing in the neighborhood known as Little Havana. Large families, a strength of Cuban society, helped their relatives find work in the growing community of Cuban exiles. Then, in the 1970's, Cubans moved into international trade, banking, and manufacturing.

Today, the Cuban influence has made Miami the center of Latin culture in the U.S. The city has three Spanish-language television stations, and supports a wide variety of Spanish radio stations, newspapers, and magazines. In 1985, Miami elected its first Cuban-American mayor, Xavier Suarez. Suarez was only 12 when his family came to the U.S.

"For Latins, it is a dream," says Adolfo Leyva, an expert on Latin America at Florida State University.

Xavier Suarez, a Cuban immigrant, finds out that
he has won the election for Miami's mayor. Suarez
is just one of many Cubans who have succeeded
in the U.S.

"Miami offers all the material advantages of American society and [also] Latin culture."

The success of Cubans in the U.S. has acted as a powerful lure to many who remain under Castro's rule. In 1980, Castro allowed 125,000 Cubans to leave for political freedom in the U.S. Known as the Marielites, these refugees crossed the Florida Strait in private boats from Mariel Harbor to Key West, Florida.

U.S. officials were angered when about 2,000 of the refugees were found to be mentally ill or to have criminal records. They charged Castro with trying to get rid of his nation's misfits. Most of the Marielites, however, are working hard to succeed in their new country.

Most Cubans who stayed behind say that life has improved under Castro's government. Housing is better. Everyone now has access to free medical services and to schools. Different foods and luxuries are easier to come by.

Julio* is a young Cuban who supports the revolution. He's 17 and wants to be a teacher. "I had to choose two subjects to specialize in, so I chose biology and soil engineering," he explains. "These are subjects which are very important in Cuba today, because we are trying to grow more kinds of crops besides sugar cane and tobacco.

"I study hard, even during vacations. That's because you have to make good grades if you want to continue with higher education. We are given progress tests every month. Our course includes two years of classroom practice. I'll spend one of these years in a city school and the other in some remote country area.

"When I am graduated, I may be sent to teach anywhere in Cuba," he says. "It will depend on where teachers are needed most."

Double-check

Review

1. By whom and when was Cuba discovered?

2. What did Castro promise to the Cuban people?

3. What reason did Castro give for saying that free elections were no longer necessary?

4. What was the Cuban Missile Crisis?

5. What will determine where in Cuba Julio may be sent to teach when he graduates?

Discussion

1. Do you think the Castro government has been better for Cuba than the Batista government was? Why, or why not? Do revolutionary governments usually end up being just as oppressive as the dictators they overthrow? Why might this happen? Is the Castro government sowing the seeds of its own eventual overthrow? Give reasons for your answers.

2. Why do you think the Cuban government outlaws dissent and protests? Is the freedom to protest against government actions important to a society? Why, or why not? Is it dangerous to a society? If so, how?

3. In 1980, about 125,000 Cubans fled their homeland and came to the United States as political refugees. Some U.S. citizens criticized the government for accepting the refugees. Others praised the U.S. for being willing to help people in need of refuge. What are your views on this matter? Explain reasons for your opinion.

Activities

1. A committee of students might prepare a bulletin board display and/or oral reports on various aspects of life in Cuba, including art, architecture, music, language, religion, dress, crafts, customs, politics, and the economy.

2. A Cuban refugee who has settled in the U.S. might be invited to speak to the class about her or his life in Cuba and in the U.S. A committee of students might prepare questions for the speaker beforehand.

3. Two (or more) students might role-play a conversation between Julio and a Cuban refugee who is studying biology in the U.S. Would they be curious about each other's lives?

Skills

Universal Press Syndicate © 1980 Washington Star

Use the political cartoon above and information in Chapter 23 to answer the following questions.

1. Whom does the man on the right represent?
   (a) Fidel Castro (b) Ronald Reagan (c) Uncle Sam

2. Who is the man on the left?
   (a) Fulgencio Batista (b) Fidel Castro (c) Ronald Reagan

3. Who are the small people rushing through the door?
   (a) Cuban refugees   (b) Cuban baseball fans   (c) orphans

4. Why does the man on the right seem surprised and confused?
   (a) He is not quite sure how he feels about all these refugees coming into his house.
   (b) He doesn't know where the baseball game is.
   (c) He didn't expect to see Castro standing there.

5. The refugees have been living under what kind of laws?
   (a) They were not allowed to attend baseball games.
   (b) They were not allowed to protest against the government.
   (c) They were required to attend church every day.

Chapter 24

Dangerous Diamonds

CUBA IS THE BEST-KNOWN of the Caribbean nations, but it is by no means the only important nation. Island nations are dotted through the Caribbean like diamonds on a necklace.

Haiti has a long and troubled history. It was colonized in 1677 by the French, who brought slaves from Africa to work their sugarcane and coffee plantations. When Haitians overthrew their French masters in 1804, they set up the world's first black republic. Haiti also became the second nation in the Western Hemisphere, after the U.S., to gain its independence.

But Haiti soon fell under the control of a small elite, which ran the nation for its own benefit. Between 1843 and 1915, Haitians were ruled by 22 dictators. U.S. Marines, sent to protect U.S. lives and property, occupied the nation from 1915 to 1934.

In 1957, Haiti fell under the control of Francois ("Papa Doc") Duvalier, a country doctor. Duvalier ruled brutally. Arrest and torture were commonplace. When Duvalier died in 1971, his 19-year-old son, Jean Claude ("Baby Doc") assumed power.

Despite some reforms, the vast majority of Haitians lived in conditions of harsh poverty. By 1985, the nation's average wage of $3 a day was the lowest in Latin America. Health care almost didn't exist for most of Haiti's people. The average Haitian could expect to live to only 50, the lowest life expectancy rate in the region. Only 29 percent of Haiti's adults could read.

After 29 years of rule by the Duvalier family, Haitians' anger came to a boil. Demonstrations against "Baby Doc" spread throughout the nation. Finally, on February 7, 1986, Duvalier fled Haiti for France. Haitians rejoiced, but tension remained as political and military leaders sought to restore order and move the country toward democracy.

Emile* is a 14-year-old farm boy who lives in the mountains of Haiti. He lives in a small village. "Father finished building our house about four years ago," he told a visitor. "It's made of cement blocks with a roof of corrugated iron.

"Mother cooks on a charcoal fire outside. There is a space of packed dirt there where she also has her corn grinder." Emile pointed to a tall wooden container with a long, smooth-ended stick that is used to pound the corn.

Emile's father has about half an acre of land on a steep slope. He grows potatoes, cabbages, carrots, bananas, and beans. The family also has a cow and a goat.

Emile has had only about three or four months of schooling, but it is more than his parents had. He is the only one in his family who can write his name.

"Sometimes I go to market with my mother," he says.

"It takes nearly all day to sell our bundle of things. Then Mother uses the money to buy such things as soap, matches, flour, bread, and sometimes clothes. Most people go barefoot, but I have a pair of shoes.

"Nearly everyone around goes to voodoo (witchcraft) ceremonies. But my father won't go to any of them, so I don't go either. We think it's just superstition."

Emile will most likely be a farmer like his father. In Haiti, few people have a chance to move upward.

The eastern two thirds of Hispaniola, the island on which Haiti is located, is Spanish-speaking. It became an independent state, the Dominican Republic, in 1844. Its capital is Santo Domingo, founded in 1496 and the oldest city in the Western Hemisphere.

Like Haiti, the Dominican Republic suffered through many turbulent years. U.S. Marines occupied the country from 1915 to 1924 to keep order. In 1930, Rafael Trujillo, the army's commander took power. He established a harsh dictatorship that lasted until his assassination in 1961. Political disorder followed, and the country teetered toward civil war.

Then, in 1965, U.S. troops once again intervened, this time to protect U.S. citizens and prevent further bloodshed. In 1966, new elections were held, and a democratic government headed by Joaquin Balaguer took office. Despite grave economic troubles over the past 20 years, the Dominican Republic's government has remained stable.

Luz Marina* is a 15-year-old Santo Domingo* girl who lives in a section of the city called Cristo Rey (Spanish for "Christ the King"). It's also the name of her school and church. She and her two brothers live with her aunt and uncle. Her mother is working in Puerto Rico, and she seldom sees her father.

"My older brothers work in a mat factory after school," Luz says. "They give most of the money to my aunt and uncle. They have five children of their own, all younger than we. Their house has six rooms. We have no bathtub or shower. There is a large public bath-house not far away."

Luz's brothers play baseball on a local team. Baseball is a special passion with the Dominican people. Many Dominican baseball players have gone on to become top major league players in the U.S.

Double-check

Review

1. What was the second country in the Western Hemisphere to obtain its independence from a European power?

2. What is the main language in Haiti?

3. Which family ruled Haiti for nearly 30 years?

4. What is the name of the island on which both Haiti and the Dominican Republic are located?

5. When did a democratic form of government come to the Dominican Republic?

Discussion

1. How is Emile's life similar to the lives of other villagers in Latin American countries described in earlier chapters? How does his life differ? Do you think Emile's life will change, now that the government of Haiti has changed? If not, why not? If so, how?

2. Every year thousands of American tourists vacation on Caribbean islands. What kinds of impressions of the island nations do you think these tourists get? What kinds of impressions do you think the tourists make on the islanders? Is such tourism good, or bad, for people such as Emile and Luz? Give reasons for your answers.

3. Many Haitian refugees who have fled to the U.S. charge that they are not given the acceptance and aid that is given to refugees from Cuba — because Cuba has a Communist government and Haiti does not. The U.S. government says that most Haitian refugees are not political refugees, and thus should not be treated the same as Cubans. What do you think? Should political refugees get special treatment? Explain your answer.

Activities

1. Committees of students might prepare bulletin board displays and/or oral reports on various aspects of life in Haiti, the Dominican Republic, and other Caribbean nations, including their art, architecture, music, language, religion, dress, crafts, customs, politics, and economies.

2. Some students might write to the tourist offices of several Caribbean nations, asking for brochures describing the facilities available. These brochures could then be displayed and their pictures of island life could be compared to the "pictures" of the island life described in the text.

3. Several students might role-play a conversation between Emile, Luz, and Julio, in which they discuss why they think the chapter on Caribbean nations has the title "Dangerous Diamonds."

Skills

PER CAPITA INCOME IN RELATION TO HEALTH AND MORTALITY RATES

	Average yearly income, per person	Average life expectancy	Infant mortality rate (per 1,000 live births)
Cuba	$840	72.4 years	25
Haiti	$300	45 years	130
Dominican Republic	$1,221	62.6 years	28.3

Source: *The 1986 World Almanac*

Use the chart above and information in Chapters 23 and 24 to answer the following questions.

1. Where does the information in this chart come from? For how many countries is information provided?

2. In which country do the most infants survive? In which country do the fewest infants survive?

3. Which country had the lowest average yearly income per person?

4. What is the average life expectancy for Cubans? What conclusions might you draw about the relationship between life expectancy and yearly income?

5. If Emile's parents had a new baby girl in 1985, how long would she be likely to live?

Chapter 25

Puerto Rico's Two Cultures

ON A MAP, the Caribbean island of Puerto Rico is much closer to South America than to North America. Geographically, Puerto Rico is clearly part of Latin America, not the U.S. Legally, however, it is tied to the United States in an unusual way. Puerto Rico is a self-governing "commonwealth" of the U.S.

Pulled between two cultures, Puerto Rico sometimes seems to have a split personality — part Latin, part U.S. For example, Puerto Rico elects its own Congress and its own governor. But its men have been drafted to fight in U.S. wars. Both Spanish and English are the official languages.

Although most Puerto Ricans are proud to be U.S. citizens, they are fiercely loyal to their Latin heritage. After all, Puerto Rico belonged to Spain for more than 400 years. Over that period, a society grew up that was not very different from that of Cuba or the Dominican Republic.

The Spaniards who first came to Puerto Rico were mainly interested in gold. They found a little, and put

Across an inlet in San Juan harbor, a new luxury hotel and an 18th-century fort stand guard.

the local Taino Indians to work digging for more. When the gold ran out, the Spaniards tried farming — or, rather, ordered the Indians to farm. After many Tainos rebelled and were killed, the Spanish brought in African slaves to work the plantations. Most Puerto Ricans today are the result of 450 years of blending of these three main strains: Spanish, African, Indian.

Originally the name Puerto Rico applied only to the fine harbor and the town that grew up around it. It means "rich port." The island was known as San Juan.* For unknown reasons, things got switched around. Now San Juan is the name of the capital city and Puerto Rico is the name of the whole country. The island itself is almost a perfect rectangle, about 35 miles wide and 100 miles long. It is part of a chain of islands formed by volcanoes in the Caribbean Sea.

☆ ☆ ☆ ☆ ☆ ☆ ☆ ☆ ☆

Julio lives on a hilly street in a new section of San Juan. His home is a three-room concrete house built in a government project. The concrete is protection against the hurricanes that occasionally howl across the island.

Julio attends a public school, where he is in the eighth grade. Although his mother hopes he will be able to attend one of the seven colleges on the island, Julio doubts that there will be enough money. At 14, he is the oldest of six children. His grandmother also lives with the family.

Julio's father works in a small electronics factory. He does skilled work and earns good wages. But the cost of most items in Puerto Rico is higher than on the U.S. mainland because many are imported. With a large family, the salary doesn't stretch far enough. Still, Julio's family is better off than many. One in five Puerto Rican workers is jobless.

An uncle of Julio's is a waiter at one of the city's tourist hotels. He has told Julio that he thinks he can get him a part-time job as a busboy next year.

It's easy for Julio to understand why close to two million tourists arrive every year on his sunny island. The weathermen claim that there are 360 days of sunshine a year. It may also rain on those days, but the sun will come out sometime.

Julio is part of two histories — U.S. and Puerto Rican. One advantage for Julio is that this produces an extra helping of holidays. As citizens of the U.S., Puerto Ricans celebrate 10 U.S. holidays such as Thanksgiving and Labor Day. Then there are nine more official Puerto Rican holidays.

☆　☆　☆　☆　☆　☆　☆　☆　☆

The extra helping of holidays is only a minor result of Puerto Rico's connection with the U.S. Spain ceded the island to the U.S. after the Spanish-American War in 1898. At that time, most Puerto Ricans welcomed the North Americans. They assumed that being part of a nearby democratic country was better than being part of a distant Spanish monarchy.

U.S. authorities began building roads and schools, and improving health care. Much needed doing, for the island was desperately poor and backward. In 1917 the U.S. Congress granted U.S. citizenship to Puerto Ricans, but it did not promise what many Puerto Ricans had expected: eventual statehood.

For years the big argument in Puerto Rican politics concerned its ties with the U.S. Should Puerto Rico try to become a state, or should it seek complete independence? While the arguments got louder, the people remained poor.

Finally a man came along with a new idea. Luis Muñoz Marín* believed that Puerto Ricans should stop arguing about their ties with the U.S. and concentrate on trying to improve conditions on the island. His political party began to win more and more seats in the island's Legislative Assembly.

Under U.S. control, the governor of Puerto Rico had always been a mainlander appointed by the U.S. President. Then in 1943, the governor recommended that Puerto Ricans be allowed to elect their own official to that office. The U.S. Congress agreed, and in 1948 the island elected its first governor—Luis Muñoz Marín. He dominated Puerto Rican politics for two decades, and served as the island's governor until 1964.

He suggested a new relationship with the U.S.: a hard-to-define form of government called a commonwealth. The island's new constitution, adopted in 1952, gives the island's citizens nearly the same say over their internal affairs as the 50 states of the U.S. But, Puerto Ricans do not vote in U.S. elections and do not pay federal income tax. Like the District of Columbia, Puerto Rico is represented in the U.S. Congress by a resident commissioner who has a voice but no vote.

Puerto Ricans do have one special privilege under their constitution. That is the right to vote to become independent of the U.S. (The U.S. Congress would also have to approve.) In election after election, however, political candidates favoring independence have won only limited support.

Puerto Ricans still argue about their relationship with the mainland U.S. But the link with the U.S. has helped give the island the Caribbean's highest standard of living. Most Puerto Ricans don't want to risk losing that prosperity.

Once-backward Puerto Rico now has many modern industries.

OPERATION BOOTSTRAP

PUERTO RICO has been called the "miracle of the Caribbean." Official visitors from all over the world have come to see for themselves how the island managed to work its economic miracle—industrialization and a better life for most people. Today Puerto Rico's per capita income—the island's total yearly income divided by the number of its people—is among the highest in Latin America. On a larger scale, Puerto Rico's per capita income of $4,250 in 1984 would rank it among the world's wealthiest 35 nations.

In the 1940's, Puerto Rico was a poverty-stricken island producing only a handful of farm products such as sugar, tobacco, and coffee. It had no special resources, such as minerals, that could be mined. It did have a pleasant climate and a people willing to work hard.

Governor Luis Muñoz Marín launched a program to put the island's resources—its climate and people—to work. He set up a government agency that people called *Fomento**, Spanish for improvement. It was to be a do-it-yourself operation planned and operated by Puerto Ricans. In English, this new push for development was called *Operation Bootstrap*.

Operation Bootstrap had two goals: to spur tourism, and to encourage businesses to open new factories on the island. With government money, Fomento built a fancy hotel to house visiting businessmen while the Fomento staff tried to persuade them to invest in Puerto Rico.

Fomento leased its hotel to Conrad Hilton, the U.S. hotel magnate, who opened it as the Caribe-Hilton. Soon the hotel was doing so well that other hotel operators bought land for resorts. Tourism eventually grew into a big business. Fomento's share of the profits helped pay for many other Operation Bootstrap projects.

At first, it was hard to convince businessmen that they could make a profit by building on the island. To encourage manufacturers, Puerto Rico promised low-interest loans and no taxes for several years. Another big plus was the island's large pool of workers willing to work for less than mainland wages. Ten new factories opened in 1947. Each year there were a few more. Thirty-seven opened in 1950. By the 1960's, new industries dotted the island.

Operation Bootstrap was not without its problems. Early on, Fomento invested heavily in oil refineries and chemical plants that never realized their potential. While officials focused on industry, farming lagged.

Still, Puerto Rico has come a long way. And in the 1980's, Puerto Ricans could point with pride to the island's growing strength as a manufacturing center for high-tech products.

Chapter 26

The Revolving Door

NEW YORK is just three hours from San Juan by jet plane. On almost any day at the San Juan airport, some families are saying *adiós** to a relative who is leaving for the mainland, while other families are welcoming back a relative who has returned from the mainland to live in Puerto Rico.

As U.S. citizens, Puerto Ricans can travel freely between the island and the U.S. mainland. Hundreds of thousands of Puerto Ricans have taken these flights, mostly to New York City. Today, there are more than twice as many Puerto Ricans in New York than there are in San Juan.

In 1984, for instance, 44,433 Puerto Ricans left the island. Of the 5.3 million Puerto Ricans in the U.S., 3.3 million live on the island and 2 million live on the mainland. People have gone to the mainland for many reasons, but most sought prosperity and change.

The traffic has never been all one way, however. Many Puerto Ricans want to return home from the mainland. But for some, the return home has not been as easy as they had hoped.

☆ ☆ ☆ ☆ ☆ ☆ ☆ ☆ ☆

"They call us *Newyoricans,*" said Luis,* a 15-year-old boy who lived his first 14 years in New Jersey. "It doesn't matter if you lived in Cincinnati or Detroit. If you lived on the mainland, they call you a Newyorican.

"They say we act as if we know everything, and that we have lost our Latin ways. Often they make fun of how we pronounce words. Most of my friends are other Newyoricans," Luis says.

Luis was an infant when his mother took the children to join their father who was working in a New Jersey oil refinery. Wages were higher than those available in Puerto Rico. The family lived in Newark for 14 years, but their dream was always to return one day to the island.   In both Newark and Puerto Rico, however, language has been a problem. On the mainland, both Luis and his sister Elena* had some difficulty in school because their English was poor. Now Elena has been dropped back a grade because her Spanish is shaky. She is in a special bilingual program her school has set up for returning Puerto Ricans.

Their younger brother Ramon was born on the mainland. He speaks almost no Spanish, and wishes the family would go "home." To him, home means New Jersey. According to government estimates, about one person in every 26 on the island was born on the mainland, like Ramon.

Luis's family lives nine miles west of San Juan in a big government development. Many of their neighbors are also Newyoricans. Although the children are somewhat unhappy, the parents are pleased to be back in Puerto Rico. Their father feels that he is treated with more dignity in Puerto Rico, and that life in New Jersey

*"Newyoricans" in Puerto Rico. Two youngsters
in San Juan check the back of a Spanish-language
New York paper for the latest baseball scores.*

was weakening family ties.

Family connections are highly important in Puerto Rico. There is much visiting back and forth among relatives. Now Luis, Elena, and Ramon live near three grandparents, numerous aunts and cousins, and several godparents.

"That is a mixed blessing," says Elena. "If I have a problem, my whole family will make it their business. Everybody will have an opinion. My aunt and my godmother are always telling me what to do. Still, I like living near my cousins. On the mainland, there was not enough family — just the five of us."

A social scientist studied a large number of people who had moved back to Puerto Rico. More than 60 per cent told him the main reason for moving back was personal family reasons.

Migration to the mainland has been an important safety valve for the island's fast-growing population. Puerto Rico already has more people per square mile than even Japan or India. Without the migration to the mainland, Puerto Rico would be even more crowded, and jobs even harder to find.

The Newyoricans are just one special group caught in the constant pull between two cultures, two languages, two economies, and two histories. No Puerto Rican can ignore the mainland even if he or she wants to. Puerto Rico's economy depends almost totally on exporting to the U.S. And oil, coal, natural gas, and half the food eaten on the island are imported from the mainland. Even a favorite food like *arroz con pollo** is half imported. The *pollo* may be a Puerto Rican chicken, but the *arroz* will have to be imported rice. More than half the island is mountainous, and not much good for farming. Each year more food has to be imported.

Thus, Puerto Rico has become a sort of processing

station for imported raw materials. Factories sponsored by Fomento turn the raw materials into manufactured goods. The products are generally shipped back to the U.S. Nearly all the business Puerto Rico does overseas is with the U.S. In fact, the island ranks eighth in the world as a buyer of U.S. goods.

Compared to the rest of Latin America, Puerto Rico is well off indeed, with a per capital income higher than most Central or South American nations. Compared to the U.S., however, the island is poor. Unemployment is at least double the U.S. rate. Despite all the successes of Operation Bootstrap, times are hard. More than half the island's people are enrolled in the federal food stamp program. About 60 per cent of the families on the island have incomes below the U.S. poverty standard.

"Comparing Puerto Rico to Latin America is like comparing Hawaii to the Far East," says former U.S. Congressman Herman Badillo, who is of Puerto Rican descent. And so Puerto Ricans make their comparisons with the U.S. Pulled between two cultures, they have built their "miracle in the Caribbean" while maintaining their Latin culture and heritage. Puerto Rico today is a land with one foot in North America and the other in Latin America.

Double-check

Review

1. What does *Puerto Rico* mean?

2. The concrete in Julio's house is protection against what?

3. As U.S. citizens, Puerto Ricans are entitled to what things?

4. What has been an important safety valve to the island's fast-growing population?

5. Oil, natural gas, and half the food eaten on the island are imported from where?

Discussion

1. If you were Puerto Rican, would you be in favor of statehood, complete independence from the U.S., or remaining a commonwealth? Give the reasons for your answer.

2. How do you feel about the apparent prejudice of Puerto Rican natives toward "Newyoricans"? Are people who have lived somewhere else generally resented by people who have lived all their lives in the same place? Do people who have lived in a variety of places seem to think that they know more than people who haven't? Explain your answers.

3. Chapter 26 points out, "Family connections are highly important in Puerto Rico"; and Elena says, "That is a mixed blessing." What are some advantages and disadvantages of large and close families? What aspects of Latin American culture might have contributed to the importance of the family? How does this compare with the role of the family in U.S. culture?

Activities

1. A committee of students might prepare a bulletin board display and/or oral reports on various aspects of life in Puerto Rico, including art, architecture, music, language, religion, dress, crafts, customs, politics, and the economy.

2. A group of students might hold a panel discussion in front of the class, during which they try to decide what they think will happen in Latin America during the next 10 years.

3. A committee of students might plan a three-month trip to Latin America for your class. They could list the countries, cities, and other locations which class members would most like to visit, and then name the archaeological sites, works of art, sporting events, and other things the class would like to see, including people they would like to meet.

Skills

POPULATION VERSUS POPULATION DENSITY

Population
(in millions)

Population
(per square mile)

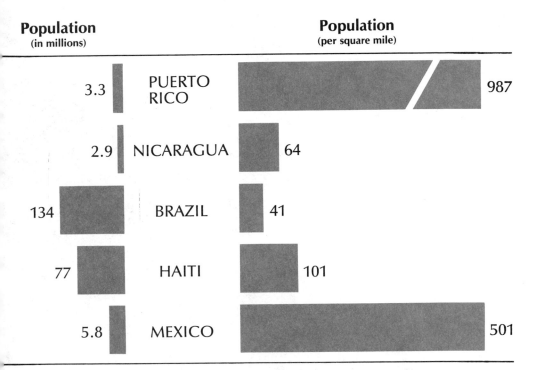

3.3	PUERTO RICO	987
2.9	NICARAGUA	64
134	BRAZIL	41
77	HAITI	101
5.8	MEXICO	501

Source: *The 1986 World Almanac*

Use the bar graph above and information in Chapters 25 and 26 to answer the following questions.

1. What do the bars on the left represent? What do the bars on the right represent?

2. Which of the above countries has the most people? The greatest density?

3. Which country might be called the least crowded?

4. About what proportion of the people in the most crowded country was born on the mainland U.S.?

5. After looking at this graph, what statement can you make about the relationship between population and population density?

Should the U.S. play the role of policeman in Latin America? In 1965 U.S. troops were sent into the Dominican Republic when a political dispute threatened to break out into bloody civil war. But, as the wall slogan indicates, not everyone welcomed the U.S. intervention.

EPILOGUE

THE U.S. AND
LATIN AMERICA

EARLY IN THE MORNING of October 25, 1983, U.S. Marines and Army Rangers invaded the small Caribbean island nation of Grenada. A few hours later, President Ronald Reagan appeared on television. He announced that the U.S. was acting to restore order, and to protect the lives of 1,000 Americans who were trapped on the island after a military takeover by Marxists inspired by the Soviet Union.

The U.S. troops ran into an unexpectedly stiff fight from Grenada's militia and 600 Cuban soldiers stationed on the island. It took several days before the U.S. invasion force of 6,000 crushed the resisters and ousted the communist regime. U. S. troops seized stores of Soviet-made weapons. President Reagan declared that Grenada had been on its way to becoming a Soviet-Cuban base ready "to export terror and undermine democracy" in the region. "We got there just in time," he said.

Six of Grenada's worried Eastern Caribbean neighbors had requested the U.S. invasion. Yet most Latin American nations denounced it. Why? The answer lies in the long and turbulent history of U.S. relations with the nations of Latin America.

For nearly 200 years, the U.S. has cast a giant shadow over its southern neighbors. That shadow has often provoked suspicion and mistrust among Latin Americans. At times, the U.S. has acted as an armed policeman, sending troops to end civil wars, restore order, and protect property. But the U.S. also has acted as a helpful big brother, promoting economic development and cooperation.

U.S. leaders have swung back and forth between those two roles since 1823. That's when U.S. President James Monroe declared the Western Hemisphere off limits to attempts by European powers to establish new colonies. Two goals prompted President Monroe to make his declaration. First, he hoped to encourage Latin Americans' rebellion against Spain. Second, he worried that European nations might use a foothold in Latin America to invade the U.S. The Monroe Doctrine, as the declaration is known, became the cornerstone of U.S. policies in the hemisphere.

Always, shifting U.S. interests helped determine U.S. actions. In the 1830's and 1840's, for example, tensions rose between the U.S. and Mexico as U.S. settlers moved west—and into Mexican territory. Then, in 1845, the U.S. annexed the Mexican province of Texas. The next year, war broke out with Mexico. U.S. troops went on to conquer California and the area of the present-day states of New Mexico and Arizona. That war left a sense of resentment among Mexicans that still affects their feelings toward the U.S.

*Staggering under his burden, a Peruvian dockworker
unloads sacks of bread donated by U.S. government.*

Beginning in the 1890's, the U.S. began to flex its muscles as a world power. And the first place it began to flex them was in its backyard—Latin America. The U.S. emerged from the Spanish-American War of 1898 in possession of Puerto Rico, which had been in control of Cuba.

The U.S.'s muscular new stance found its most forceful believer in President Theodore Roosevelt. He had become a war hero in the fight against Spain, leaving a top government job to lead a volunteer Cavalry regiment, known as the Rough Riders, to a key victory in Cuba.

In 1904, President Roosevelt said that the U.S. had the right and duty to act as an international policeman in the Western Hemisphere "in flagrant cases of wrongdoing or impotence." His willingness to use force was termed "big-stick diplomacy," after a famous remark Roosevelt had made. "I have always been fond of the West African proverb," he said. "Speak softly and carry a big stick, you will go far."

At different times, the U.S. sent its forces into Panama, the Dominican Republic, Haiti, Nicaragua, and Mexico in efforts to control chaotic political and economic situations. But Latin Americans objected to big stick diplomacy. They saw U.S. military intervention as a violation of their right to control their own affairs.

In the 1930's, President Franklin D. Roosevelt tried to improve relations. "I would dedicate this nation to the policy of the good neighbor," he said. He withdrew U.S. troops from the Caribbean and worked to increase cooperation between North and South America. In 1948, the U.S. and 20 Latin American nations formed the Organization of American States (OAS).

Following World War II, however, U.S. attention focused on its competition with the Soviet Union. U.S. officials gave the problems of Latin America a low priority.

Cuba's revolution in 1959 and its swing to Soviet-style communism shocked U.S. leaders. Partly to keep revolutions from sweeping through Latin America, the U.S. began a new push to help strengthen the region. In 1961, President John F. Kennedy launched an ambitious 10-year program called the "Alliance for Progress." In the early years, the U.S. sent $1 billion a year to Latin America. The Alliance urged reforms and better living standards.

Despite massive aid, the OAS produced mixed results. Brazil reaped immense benefits. In Central America, on the other hand, the Alliance brought few reforms. Economic failures and political upheavals forced nations there to lurch from crisis to crisis.

Today, Latin America is once again a top concern of U.S. officials. They are cheered by the region's overall shift away from military regimes, and the growing strength of democracy. Still, as the invasion of Grenada showed, they remain worried about possible communist gains. One thing is certain. Latin America's importance to the U.S.—as a market for our goods, and as political allies—is growing. That means U.S. policymakers will face tough choices in the years ahead as they work to strengthen southern friendships.

Pronunciation Guide

Acámbaro — ah-CAHM-bah-roh
achote — ah-CHOH-tay
Aconcagua — ak-uhn-KAHG-wuh
adíos — ah-dee-OHS
Salvador Allende — sal-bah-DOHR eye-YEN-day
arroz con pollo — ah-ROHS con POY-yoh
asado — ah-SAH-tho
Atahualpa — at-ah-WAL-pah

Herman Badillo — HER-man bah-DEE-oh
Vasco Nuñez de Balboa — BAS-coh NUN-yeth day
    bahl-BOH-ah
bandeirantes — bahn-day-RAHN-teez
Fulgencio Batista — full-HEN-see-oh bah-TEE-stah
Santa Fé de Bogotá — san-tah FAY day boh-goh-TAH
Simón Bolívar — see-MOHN boh-LEE-var
Brasilia — brah-ZEEL-yah
Buenos Aires — BWAY-nohs EYE-rayz

Cabral — kuh-BRAL
cacao — cah-COW
campesino — cam-puh-SEE-noh
Caracas — cah-RAH-cahs
Carnaval — CAR-nuh-val
Cartagena — car-teh-HAY-nah
charros — CHAH-roz
Chibcha — CHIB-chah
Chichén Itzá — chee-CHEHN eat-SAH
Colón — koh-LOHN
conquistadores — kun-KEY-stuh-doh-rez
Hernan Cortes — air-NAHN cor-TEZ
Miguel Hidalgo y Costilla — mee-GWELL
    ee-DAHL-go ee coh-STEE-yuh
cruzeiro — cru-ZAI-roh
Cuzco — COOZ-coh

Darío — dah-REE-oh
Porfirio Díaz — por-FEE-ree-oh DEE-ahz
Dolores — doh-LOW-rase

Edi — AY-dee

Elena — eh-LAY-nah
Emile — AY-meal

favelas — fah-VEL-ahs
fiesta — fee-ESS-tah
Fomento — foe-MEN-toe

Guaraní — gwah-rah-NEE
gaucho — GOW-choh

hacienda — ah-see-EN-dah

Iguassú — ee-gwah-SOO
Iquitos — ee-KEY-tos

João — zhoo-WOW
José — ho-ZAY
Josefina — ho-seh-FEE-nah
Benito Juarez — beh-NEE-toh WAR-ez
Julio — HOO-lee-oh

Lima — LEE-muh
llama — l'-YAH-mah
Luis — loo-EES
Luz Marina — LOOS mah-REE-nah

machetes — may-SHEH-tayz
Machu Picchu — MAH-choo PEE-choo
mañana — mahn-YAH-nah
Las Mañanitas — lahs mahn-yah-NEE-tahs
Maracaibo — mah-rah-KIGH-boh
María — mah-REE-ah
Luis Muñoz Marín — loo-EES MOON-yos mah-REEN
matador — MAH-tah-dore
maté — mah-TAY
Mayans — MY-unz
Mérida — MEH-ree-dah
mestizos — meh-STEE-zohz
Miguel — mee-GWELL
Minas Gerais –– MEE-nahs zhuh-RICE
Moctezuma — mok-teh-SOO-mah
Montaña — mohn-TAN-yah
Montevideo — mon-tuh-vuh-DAY-oh

olé — oh-LAY

Pampa — PAHM-pah
paseo — pah-SAY-oh
Paseo de la Reforma — pah-SAY-oh day lah
    ray-FOR-mah
pau brasil — pow brah-ZEEL
Juan Perón — WAHN pay-ROAN
Peronistas — pay-roan-EES-tuhs
Francisco Pizarro — frahn-SEEZ-koh pee-ZAH-roh
Plaza de Armas — PLAH-sah day AR-mahz
porteño — por-TAYN-yoh
La Prensa — lah PREN-sah
Punta del Este — PUN-tah dell ESS-tay

Quechua — KECH-wuh
Gonzalo Jiminez de Quesada — gon-ZAH-low
    hee-MEN-eth day kay-SAH-dah
Quetzalcoatl — ket-SAHL-kwaht-'l
Quito — KEY-toh

Ramon — rah-MOHN
rayola — ray-OH-lay
Rio Grande — REE-oh GRAHN-day
Rio de Janeiro — REE-oo dih zhuh-NAY-roo

San Juan — san HWAHN
José de San Martín — ho-ZAY day san mar-TEEN
Santiago — san-tee-AH-go
Santo Domingo — SAN-toe do-MEEN-go
São Paulo — SOW POW-loo
Severino — seh-vuh-REE-noh
Sierra Maestra — see-AIR-uh my-ACE-truh
siesta — see-ESS-tuh
Somoza — suh-MOE-zuh

El Teniente — ell ten-YEN-tay
Tenochtitlán — tah-noch-tet-LAHN
tortillas — tor-TEE-yuhs
Los Tres Reyes — lohs trayz RAY-eez

Getulio Vargas — zhuh-TOO-lee-oo VAR-gahs
Pancho Villa — PAN-choh VEE-yuh
Heitor Villa-Lobos — ay-TOR VILL-ah LOH-bos

Yucatán — you-kah-TAHN

Index

*Photograph.

235